AMERICA'S
TEST KITCHEN

also by the editors at america's test kitchen

Cooking at Home with Bridget and Julia
The Complete Slow Cooker
The Complete Make-Ahead Cookbook
The Complete Mediterranean Cookbook
The Complete Vegetarian Cookbook
The Complete Cooking for Two Cookbook
Just Add Sauce
How to Roast Everything
Nutritious Delicious
What Good Cooks Know
Cook's Science
The Science of Good Cooking
The Perfect Cake
The Perfect Cookie
Bread Illustrated
Dinner Illustrated
Master of the Grill
Kitchen Smarts
Kitchen Hacks
100 Recipes: The Absolute Best Ways to Make the True Essentials
The New Family Cookbook
The America's Test Kitchen Cooking School Cookbook
The Cook's Illustrated Meat Book
The Cook's Illustrated Baking Book
The Cook's Illustrated Cookbook
The America's Test Kitchen Family Baking Book
The Best of America's Test Kitchen (2007–2018 Editions)
The Complete America's Test Kitchen TV Show Cookbook 2001–2018

Food Processor Perfection
Pressure Cooker Perfection
Vegan for Everybody
Naturally Sweet
Foolproof Preserving
Paleo Perfected
The How Can It Be Gluten-Free Cookbook: Volume 2
The How Can It Be Gluten-Free Cookbook
The Best Mexican Recipes
Slow Cooker Revolution Volume 2: The Easy-Prep Edition
Slow Cooker Revolution
The Six-Ingredient Solution
The America's Test Kitchen D.I.Y. Cookbook

THE COOK'S ILLUSTRATED ALL-TIME BEST SERIES
All-Time Best Sunday Suppers
All-Time Best Holiday Entertaining
All-Time Best Appetizers
All-Time Best Soups

COOK'S COUNTRY TITLES
One-Pan Wonders
Cook It in Cast Iron
Cook's Country Eats Local
The Complete Cook's Country TV Show Cookbook

FOR A FULL LISTING OF ALL OUR BOOKS
CooksIllustrated.com
AmericasTestKitchen.com

praise for other america's test kitchen titles

"This book upgrades slow cooking for discriminating, 21st-century palates—that is indeed revolutionary."
THE DALLAS MORNING NEWS ON *SLOW COOKER REVOLUTION*

"This book begins with a detailed buying guide, a critical summary of available sizes and attachments, and a list of clever food processor techniques. Easy and versatile dishes follow . . . Both new and veteran food processor owners will love this practical guide."
LIBRARY JOURNAL ON *FOOD PROCESSOR PERFECTION*

"Another winning cookbook from ATK. . . . The folks at America's Test Kitchen apply their rigorous experiments to determine the facts about these pans."
BOOKLIST ON *COOK IT IN CAST IRON*

"A terrifically accessible and useful guide to grilling in all its forms that sets a new bar for its competitors on the bookshelf. . . . The book is packed with practical advice, simple tips, and approachable recipes."
PUBLISHERS WEEKLY (STARRED REVIEW) ON *MASTER OF THE GRILL*

"This encyclopedia of meat cookery would feel completely overwhelming if it weren't so meticulously organized and artfully designed. This is Cook's Illustrated at its finest."
THE KITCHN ON *THE COOK'S ILLUSTRATED MEAT BOOK*

Selected as the Cookbook Award Winner of 2017 in the Baking Category
INTERNATIONAL ASSOCIATION OF CULINARY PROFESSIONALS (IACP) ON *BREAD ILLUSTRATED*

"With 1,000 photos and the expertise of the America's Test Kitchen editors, this title might be the definitive book on bread baking."
PUBLISHERS WEEKLY ON *BREAD ILLUSTRATED*

"The editors at America's Test Kitchen pack decades of baking experience into this impressive volume of 250 recipes. . . . You'll find a wealth of keeper recipes within these pages."
LIBRARY JOURNAL (STARRED REVIEW) ON *THE PERFECT COOKIE*

Selected as one of Amazon's Best Books of 2015 in the Cookbooks and Food Writing Category
AMAZON ON *THE COMPLETE VEGETARIAN COOKBOOK*

"Cooks with a powerful sweet tooth should scoop up this well-researched recipe book for healthier takes on classic sweet treats."
BOOKLIST ON *NATURALLY SWEET*

"The 21st-century *Fannie Farmer Cookbook* or *The Joy of Cooking*. If you had to have one cookbook and that's all you could have, this one would do it."
CBS SAN FRANCISCO ON *THE NEW FAMILY COOKBOOK*

"The go-to gift book for newlyweds, small families, or empty nesters."
ORLANDO SENTINEL ON *THE COMPLETE COOKING FOR TWO COOKBOOK*

"The sum total of exhaustive experimentation . . . anyone interested in gluten-free cookery simply shouldn't be without it."
NIGELLA LAWSON ON *THE HOW CAN IT BE GLUTEN-FREE COOKBOOK*

"A one-volume kitchen seminar, addressing in one smart chapter after another the sometimes surprising whys behind a cook's best practices. . . . You get the myth, the theory, the science, and the proof, all rigorously interrogated as only America's Test Kitchen can do."
NPR ON *THE SCIENCE OF GOOD COOKING*

"The perfect kitchen home companion. . . . The practical side of things is very much on display . . . cook-friendly and kitchen-oriented, illuminating the process of preparing food instead of mystifying it."
THE WALL STREET JOURNAL ON *THE COOK'S ILLUSTRATED COOKBOOK*

MULTICOOKER PERFECTION

Cook It Fast or Cook It Slow—You Decide

the Editors at America's Test Kitchen

Instant Pot® is a registered trademark of the Instant Pot Company.
Crock-Pot® is a registered trademark of Newell Brands.
GoWISE USA® is a registered trademark of Ming's Mark Inc.
Fagor Lux™ is an unregistered trademark of Fagor America Inc.

Library of Congress Cataloging-in-Publication Data

Names: America's Test Kitchen (Firm)
Title: Multicooker perfection : cook it fast or cook it slow-you decide /
    by the editors at America's Test Kitchen.
Description: Boston, MA : America's Test Kitchen, 2018. | Includes index.
Identifiers: LCCN 2017055683 | ISBN 9781945256288 (paperback)
Subjects: LCSH: Pressure cooking. | Electric cooking, Slow. | Cooking. |
    BISAC: COOKING / Methods / Special Appliances. | COOKING /
    Methods / General. | COOKING / Methods / Quick & Easy. |
    LCGFT: Cookbooks.
Classification: LCC TX840.P7 M85 2018 | DDC 641.5/87--dc23
LC record available at https://lccn.loc.gov/2017055683

AMERICA'S TEST KITCHEN
21 Drydock Avenue, Boston, MA 02210
Manufactured in Canada
10 9 8 7 6 5 4 3 2 1

Distributed by Penguin Random House Publisher Services
Tel: 800.733.3000

Pictured on front cover: Vietnamese Beef Pho (page 26), Chinese
Barbecued Spareribs (page 119), Teriyaki Chicken Thighs with Carrots
and Snow Peas (page 67), Cider-Braised Pork Pot Roast (page 112),
Poached Salmon with Cucumber and Tomato Salad (page 87), Parmesan
Risotto (page 137)

Pictured on back cover (counterclockwise from top): Meatballs and
Marinara (page 78), Cheesecake (page 172), Easy Beef Stew (page 32),
Braised Chicken Breasts with Tomatoes and Capers (page 59), Shredded
Pork Soft Tacos (page 114)

Chief Creative Officer JACK BISHOP

Editorial Director, Books ELIZABETH CARDUFF

Executive Editor JULIA COLLIN DAVISON

Executive Editor ADAM KOWIT

Executive Food Editor DAN ZUCCARELLO

Senior Editor ANNE WOLF

Associate Editors LEAH COLINS, MELISSA DRUMM, AND RUSSELL SELANDER

Test Cook KATHRYN CALLAHAN

Editorial Assistant ALYSSA LANGER

Design Director, Books CAROLE GOODMAN

Deputy Art Directors ALLISON BOALES AND JEN KANAVOS HOFFMAN

Designer KATIE BARRANGER

Production Designer REINALDO CRUZ

Photography Director JULIE BOZZO COTE

Photography Producers MARY BALL AND MEREDITH MULCAHY

Senior Staff Photographer DANIEL J. VAN ACKERE

Staff Photographer STEVE KLISE AND KEVIN WHITE

Photography KELLER + KELLER AND CARL TREMBLAY

Food Styling CATRINE KELTY, CHANTAL LAMBETH, KENDRA MCKNIGHT,
MARIE PIRAINO, ELLE SIMONE SCOTT, AND SALLY STAUB

Photoshoot Kitchen Team

        Manager TIMOTHY MCQUINN

        Lead Test Cook DANIEL CELLUCCI

        Assistant Test Cooks MADY NICHAS AND JESSICA RUDOLPH

Illustration JAY LAYMAN

Production Director GUY ROCHFORD

Senior Production Manager JESSICA LINDHEIMER QUIRK

Production Manager CHRISTINE SPANGER

Imaging Manager LAUREN ROBBINS

Production and Imaging Specialists HEATHER DUBE, DENNIS NOBLE,
AND JESSICA VOAS

Copy Editor JEFF SCHIER

Proofreader PAT JALBERT-LEVINE

Indexer ELIZABETH PARSON

CONTENTS

WELCOME TO AMERICA'S TEST KITCHEN

This book has been tested, written, and edited by the folks at America's Test Kitchen. Located in Boston's Seaport District in the historic Innovation and Design Building, it features 15,000 square feet of kitchen space including multiple photography and video studios. It is the home of *Cook's Illustrated* magazine and *Cook's Country* magazine and is the workday destination for more than 60 test cooks, editors, and cookware specialists. Our mission is to test recipes over and over again until we understand how and why they work and until we arrive at the best version.

We start the process of testing a recipe with a complete lack of preconceptions, which means that we accept no claim, no technique, and no recipe at face value. We simply assemble as many variations as possible, test a half-dozen of the most promising, and taste the results blind. We then construct our own recipe and continue to test it, varying ingredients, techniques, and cooking times until we reach a consensus. As we like to say in the test kitchen, "We make the mistakes so you don't have to." The result, we hope, is the best version of a particular recipe, but we realize that only you can be the final judge of our success (or failure). We use the same rigorous approach when we test equipment and taste ingredients.

All of this would not be possible without a belief that good cooking, much like good music, is based on a foundation of objective technique. Some people like spicy foods and others don't, but there is a right way to sauté, there is a best way to cook a pot roast, and there are measurable scientific principles involved in producing perfectly beaten, stable egg whites. Our ultimate goal is to investigate the fundamental principles of cooking to give you the techniques, tools, and ingredients you need to become a better cook. It is as simple as that.

To see what goes on behind the scenes at America's Test Kitchen, check out our social media channels for kitchen snapshots, exclusive content, video tips, and much more. You can watch us work (in our actual test kitchen) by tuning in to *America's Test Kitchen* or *Cook's Country from America's Test Kitchen* on public television or on our websites. Listen in to test kitchen experts on public radio (SplendidTable.org) to hear insights that illuminate the truth about real home cooking. Want to hone your cooking skills or finally learn how to bake—with an America's Test Kitchen test cook? Enroll in one of our online cooking classes. However you choose to visit us, we welcome you into our kitchen, where you can stand by our side as we test our way to the best recipes in America.

facebook.com/AmericasTestKitchen
twitter.com/TestKitchen
youtube.com/AmericasTestKitchen
instagram.com/TestKitchen
pinterest.com/TestKitchen
google.com/+AmericasTestKitchen

AmericasTestKitchen.com
CooksIllustrated.com
CooksCountry.com
OnlineCookingSchool.com

MULTICOOKER 101

INTRODUCTION

Multicookers like the Instant Pot are getting more popular by the day. Legions of devoted fans sing the praises of these electric pressure cooking/slow cooking/rice cooking/yogurt making devices. For busy families, the appeal is undeniable: These appliances promise to make getting dinner on the table faster and easier than ever. Hassle-free home-cooked meals? We were drawn in by the potential.

Most multicooker recipes out there make use of only the pressure cook setting of these versatile machines. Why limit them, we thought, when they can do so much more? Plus, most speak to only one brand of multicooker. So, like every project we take on here at America's Test Kitchen, we aimed to set the bar higher, and to offer more for the home cook. Our ambitious, multifaceted goal: develop simple, flavorful, and absolutely bullet-proof multicooker recipes that would work in any brand of multicooker. Most of all, we wanted every recipe to work on both the pressure cook setting and the slow cook setting. One ingredient list, one dish, two ways to cook.

It quickly became apparent why these machines have such a following. The built-in sauté function meant we never had to turn on the stove, so there were fewer dishes to wash. We could pressure cook recipes that would normally take hours in far less time. And having to store only one appliance (versus three or four) was certainly advantageous.

But with all their benefits came their inevitable challenges. Before we started developing recipes, we spent several weeks running temperature tests on all the models. Our conclusion: All multicookers work slightly differently. These inconsistencies were most apparent when using the slow cook function: The Instant Pot, a brand that is owned (and loved) by millions of people (including a large percentage of our surveyed readers), and that worked perfectly on the pressure setting, simply couldn't keep up on the slow cook setting. It was this finding, along with the pot's popularity, that led us to our exhaustive recipe testing protocol: Not only did we test every recipe in our winning multicooker, the Fagor LUX LCD, we also tested every recipe on both the pressure and the slow cook settings in the Instant Pot, and incorporated special instructions in the recipes where needed. It was a lot of work, but it guaranteed that our recipes worked for everyone.

The end results were well worth our efforts, and we couldn't be more pleased with the foolproof recipes we offer here. We're putting you in the driver's seat: If you need to get dinner

on the table ASAP, you can choose the pressure cook instructions. If you prefer to prep in advance so your food cooks while you're out, you can opt for the slow cook setting.

So what are the recipes you will find here? All kinds, from comforting Chicken Noodle Soup that utilizes a whole chicken, to a Cider-Braised Pork Pot Roast that's impressive enough for company. Tasters couldn't get enough of our supersimple Macaroni and Cheese (the secret is melty Monterey Jack cheese) or the deep flavors of our classic Meatballs and Marinara. When you want to go beyond dinner, check out "Ten Unexpected Things to Make in Your Multicooker" (page 153), where you'll find a killer cheesecake (we cover the pan so condensation doesn't mar the top of the cake) and perfect Buffalo wings (the multicooker does a great job of moderating the temperature of the frying oil).

In the pages that follow, you'll find a guide to successful multicooking. We recommend reading this section before you dive into cooking, whether you've been using your multicooker for years or haven't taken it out of its box yet.

COOKING FAST—OR SLOW

Every recipe in this book gives you options for both pressure cooking and slow cooking, so you can choose which works for you. To further help you plan, we've included the total time using either method. Those times include tasks like prepping ingredients, sautéing aromatics, and bringing the pot up to pressure, so you'll know just when you can expect dinner to be ready.

When using the pressure setting, note that the time we give in the recipe (for example, "Select high pressure cook function and cook for 10 minutes") is the time you should set on your multicooker's timer. The multicooker will automatically start the cooking timer when the pot reaches pressure (which can take as few as 5 minutes or as long as 30 minutes, depending on what's in the pot).

A final note: Because the Instant Pot, when used on the slow cook function, runs at a much lower temperature than other multicookers (see pages 7 and 8), we often needed to make adjustments in our recipes. This might be as simple as switching from low to high; sometimes we also increased the time range. In a few cases, we found that food simply wouldn't become fully tender on the Instant Pot slow setting, though we still got excellent results when using the pressure cook function. Be sure to read through the recipe completely before you begin; any necessary adjustments will be called out in the recipe.

WHY YOU SHOULD OWN A MULTICOOKER

Multicookers are one of the most versatile appliances you can own—the proof is right there in the name. But if you're still not convinced, here are a few more reasons we think that every kitchen should be equipped with one:

1 **You end up with fewer dishes to wash.** One of the best features about a multicooker is that you can sauté, brown, and simmer right in the pot—there's no need to dirty another pan to brown ingredients before cooking.

2 **They're foolproof.** Many multicookers offer intuitive controls, and the lid locks on easily. They maintain pressure and/or heat without any monitoring required. If you follow the recipes in this book closely, you'll get perfect results every time—no need to worry about your oven not being properly calibrated, or your stovetop burner running too hot.

3 **They're safe.** Everyone has heard stories about exploding pressure cookers and meals that ended up on the kitchen ceiling instead of on the dinner plates. Not so with multicookers. These appliances have multiple safety features that allow any excess pressure to escape safely—and without creating a mess.

4 **They put more options on the table for week-night meals.** Multicookers are ideal for the cook who is short on time but doesn't want to be limited to quick recipes, frozen meals, and takeout. A multicooker makes braises, stews, and numerous other traditionally long-cooked meals a viable weeknight option, whether you're pressure cooking the recipe quickly or letting it cook slowly until you're ready to eat.

5 **Dishes have more flavor.** Pressure cooking translates to maximum flavor because the volatile flavor molecules can't escape the enclosed environment as they do from traditional stovetop cookware. Basically, the sealed pot means more flavor stays in the food. This also means pressure cooking is great for making stock.

6 **They help keep your kitchen cool and odor-free.** The heat and the flavor stay in the pot, so your kitchen remains cool and food smells don't permeate the air.

GETTING TO KNOW YOUR MULTICOOKER

Multicookers contain more than meets the eye. Every piece, valve, and button plays an important role in making the machine work properly, so it's a good idea to familiarize yourself with the basic parts before you start cooking. Not all multicookers look the same, but most are made up of similar parts. The drawing at right illustrates our winning multicooker, the Fagor LUX LCD; see your manual for specific information and language for your model.

While our winning multicooker doesn't come with any extra inserts or pieces, some multicookers do include steamer baskets, rice paddles, and more. We don't use these pieces in our recipes; refer to your manual for correct use.

1 pressure regulating knob/steam release valve
When you're cooking under pressure, this valve must be closed or turned to "pressure." When slow cooking, this valve needs to be open to allow steam to escape (thereby not building up pressure in the pot). When opening the valve after pressure cooking, be sure to shield your hand with a towel or oven mitt, as the steam will be hot.

2 floating valve
This valve controls the amount of pressure in the pot by allowing excess pressure to be released during cooking.

3 safety pressure valve
The safety pressure valve works independent of the floating valve, but it also allows excess pressure to escape during pressure cooking.

4 silicone gasket
This rubber ring fits snugly in a channel around the perimeter of the underside of the lid. When the lid is in place correctly, the gasket creates an airtight seal, which in turn allows pressure to build within the pot.

5 lid
The lid is specially designed to create an airtight seal with the help of the silicone gasket (#4), when properly locked in place on the pot.

6 locked lid indicator/self-locking pin/lid position mark
This indicator is activated during pressure cooking to let you know that the lid is locked. You will not be able to open the lid when it is locked, since doing so could be dangerous.

7 heating element
The heating element regulates the temperature in the pot for all functions, including pressure cooking, slow cooking, and sautéing or browning.

8 removable cooking pot
The cooking pots are made of aluminum or stainless steel, and may or may not have a nonstick coating. All food should be cooked in this pot. Note: Pay attention to the fill lines. Do not overfill the pot, as this can cause food to cook improperly, or, worse, result in valve blockages that could cause the pot to malfunction.

9 base/stationary pot/cooker housing
This is simply the base of the multicooker, where the removable pot sits and where the control panel and all of the electronics are housed.

10 control panel
This is where you control all of the functions of your multicooker. Each cooker varies in the buttons it offers and how to set each function, but all will have an option (or two) for pressure cooking, slow cooking, and browning and/or sautéing. The control panel will also show you when the pot comes up to pressure and allow you to set a cook timer.

- **pressure cook setting** Most multicookers will have the option for "high" and "low" pressure cooking. We most often use high pressure. See page 12 for more information about pressure cooking.

- **slow cook setting** Many multicookers will have the option for "high" and "low" slow cooking, though some have only one slow cook option. See page 14 for more information about slow cooking.

- **brown/sear/sauté setting** When browning meat, blooming aromatics, or reducing a sauce after pressure or slow cooking, we use this function. Because the heating element of a multicooker isn't as efficient as a stove burner, we always use the hottest setting for the most effective cooking. The hottest function is sometimes called brown, high sauté, sear, etc. Check your manual to figure out what yours is.

- **other buttons and settings** Note that some multicookers offer specific settings for food such as meat, soup, and risotto. Usually, these are just variations on the pressure or slow settings, sometimes with built-in timing. We don't use these settings in this book, since they vary by appliance and therefore are not as reliable as using the regular pressure or slow settings and following our recipes for temperature and timing.

TESTING MULTICOOKERS

If you've been online lately, you probably already know that people are downright fanatical about Instant Pot, a brand of multicooker that's taking the Internet by storm. There are countless blogs dedicated to these cookers. The most popular Instant Pot Facebook group has more than 725,000 members and is growing by the thousands each week. Amazon's 2017 Prime Day was the biggest sales day in company history; the top-selling product in both the United States and Canada, after Amazon devices? The Instant Pot.

Part of the genius is the name. Instant Pot sounds convenient and approachable, so even though it's really just an electric pressure cooker with additional features, unlike regular pressure cookers its name doesn't connote dangerous explosions (though pressure cookers are quite safe these days). The company's other brilliant move: eschewing traditional advertising in favor of handing out complimentary units to bloggers and letting them and social media do the rest. Personal stories and word of mouth are powerful, and they've created a community that people want in on.

The appeal of multicookers is undeniable: one appliance to buy, store, and understand versus multiple. But Instant Pot is not the only brand of multicooker available. Was it really the best option? We tested six multicooker models priced from $79.99 to $199.95, including the best-selling Instant Pot model. After nearly 100 pounds of meat, 20 pounds of beans, and five weeks of testing, would we agree with the hoards of fans?

Pressure Cooking in a Multicooker

We started by evaluating the pressure cooking function on each machine. Pressure cookers are essentially just extremely tightly sealed pots. The boiling point of water is higher in a closed environment because the pressure makes it harder for the water to turn to steam; this is why pressure cookers can cook food faster. And because the pot stays closed and so loses hardly any moisture, you can use less liquid and the flavors become more concentrated.

All of the machines except for one made great pressure-cooked food. Chuck-eye roast was meltingly tender after just 25 minutes, bone-in chicken breasts were juicy and fully cooked in 17 minutes, and presoaked dried beans were creamy but intact in 50 minutes. The one model that failed, from Aobosi, had a droopy gasket that repeatedly prevented it from sealing correctly; an identical model performed similarly, and even though it's a top seller on Amazon, the company was incommunicado when we reached out to customer service.

To understand what was going on inside the multicookers while they cooked under pressure, we filled each with a precise amount of water and used a wireless temperature tracker to see how hot they got on both their low and high pressure settings; the hotter the temperature, the higher the pressure. None of them got as hot as a stovetop pressure cooker, which reaches around 250 degrees and 15 psi (pounds per square inch) on high, compared to 212 degrees, the boiling point of water in a regular pot. This means multicookers will cook slightly slower than stovetop pressure cookers, though still much faster than other cooking methods.

After coming up to pressure, all of the multicookers performed similarly on low pressure. But most of the time we use high pressure because it's more efficient. Here, the Instant Pot was an outlier: It took longer to come up to pressure, and once it did it cooked slightly hotter, at 246.5 degrees, compared to 235 to 240 degrees for the others. Luckily, this makes a difference only for delicate foods like chicken breasts, and if you tweak cooking times, you can get good pressure cooked food out of it. (In this book, we've added instructions for how to adjust recipes, reducing times slightly for the Instant Pot where necessary.)

HIGH PRESSURE ISN'T ALWAYS EQUAL

Most of the time we use the high pressure setting because it's more efficient. Most models we tested performed fairly similarly to our winner, the Fagor LUX LCD, which reaches its maximum temperature of 238 degrees in about 20 minutes. But the Instant Pot worked slightly differently: It took about 25 minutes to reach its maximum temperature of about 247 degrees, meaning it took longer to come to pressure and then cooked hotter. We found this mattered only for delicate foods like chicken breasts, and slightly tweaking cooking times ensured good results.

■ Fagor LUX LCD
■ Instant Pot Duo

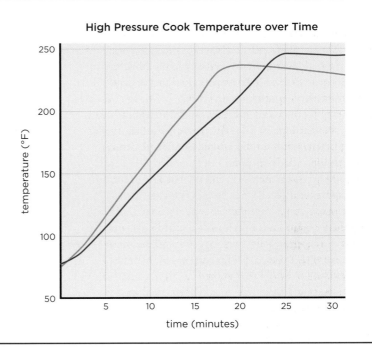

High Pressure Cook Temperature over Time

What About Rice in a Multicooker?

Multicookers also promise to replace rice cookers. Typically we cook rice on the stove, in the oven, or in a rice cooker. In all of these methods, part of the water gets absorbed and the rest evaporates. But multicookers pressure cook the rice, with very little evaporation, so all of the water gets concentrated and absorbed. This made for a stickier final product; however, all of the models except the one with the sealing issue made acceptable white or brown rice, though we had to tweak manufacturers' recipes (if they even had them) to get optimal results.

Searing Lessons Learned

It's nice not to have to dirty an additional pot if you want to sauté onions or cook down wine to kick off your dish, so we examined how well multicookers handled such tasks. The Instant Pot has three specific sauté settings (low, medium, and high), while most other models have a single "sauté" button. When we sautéed onions on high in the Instant Pot, it did fairly well. But with the other models we waited. And waited some more. Some units took upward of an hour to cook one measly onion. After we had played around with the appliances for a while, we learned that many of them have a second setting, typically labeled "brown," that functions like a skillet. Intended to sear meat, this setting is hotter and gave us better results, allowing us to sauté and sear in a more timely manner.

Slow Cooking In A Multicooker

We were feeling pretty good about these devices overall—until we tried to slow cook. Here, we encountered two problems. The first had to do with multicookers in general: They work very differently than traditional slow cookers because they heat up really fast, while a slow cooker gently warms to its target temperature.

This is a problem with foods that are more delicate, such as chicken breasts, because those foods will overcook if you try to use a general slow cooker recipe, one that isn't specifically designed for a multicooker's more aggressive heating. But we found we could surmount this problem by reducing cook times. For example, a chicken dish made using the multicooker's slow cooking function typically took about an hour less than when we made the same recipe in our winning traditional slow cooker. When we used adapted recipes as opposed to ones specific to slow cookers, all of the multicookers we tested were able to produce nicely juicy chicken.

Our second slow cooking problem, however, proved more challenging. Uneven cooking happened to an extent in all of the multicookers during our slow cooking tests. The food on the bottom of the inserts tended to cook faster than the food at the top. The location of the heating elements and the shape of the inserts played a role here.

In a multicooker, the heating element is set below the insert (much as a pot sits on a stovetop burner), while in some slow cookers, like our favorite, the heating element wraps around the perimeter of the pot like a belt. All of the multicookers had taller pots (6 to 7 inches high) with narrower cooking surfaces (8 to 8.5 inches in diameter), compared to our winning slow cooker, which is shallower (only 4.5 inches tall) with a broader oval-shaped cooking surface (10.9 by 6.8 inches wide). In a taller, narrower multicooker, the food is piled higher so the heat has to travel farther, 6 to 7 inches upward, to reach all the food. In a slow cooker, with its broader pot, the food is shallower and the heat encircles it, so the heat has to travel only 3 inches or so at most to penetrate the food.

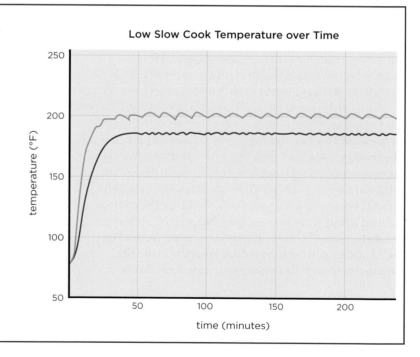

SOMETIMES, LOW SLOW IS TOO LOW

For most models, including our winner, the Fagor LUX LCD, we use the low slow cook function to cook food gently. But when we performed water temperature tests, we found that the Instant Pot's low slow setting was significantly lower than that of most models, running at only 187 degrees compared to our winner's 204 degrees. For this reason, when using the Instant Pot on the slow cook function, we always use the high setting, which cooks at about 206 degrees.

▪ Fagor LUX LCD
■ Instant Pot Duo

Low Slow Cook Temperature over Time

temperature (°F) vs. time (minutes)

To understand all of the machines' heating patterns during slow cooking, we heated precisely 5 pounds of water in each on the low setting for 5 hours. On low, the Instant Pot was drastically cooler. It topped out at 186.7 degrees, compared to 198 to 207.9 degrees in most of the others—an 11.3- to 21.2-degree difference.

To give the Instant Pot the best possible chance for success, we adjusted and slow-cooked everything in it on high during testing. But even then it still lagged behind the rest. It maxed out at 206.2 degrees in the water test, compared to 207.9 to 214.1 degrees in most of the other models, a 1.7- to 7.9-degree difference. And heat moves more easily through water than through denser mediums, which explains why we saw the Instant Pot fail with thicker, large-volume recipes like Easy Beef Stew and Chili con Carne. These took up to 16 hours in the Instant Pot, meaning you'd have to start your machine at 4 a.m. to have dinner ready by 8 p.m. And even after 16 hours, some dishes, such as Chinese Barbecued Spareribs, were still not fully cooked.

To figure out why the Instant Pot was slower than other models, we contacted Dr. Robert A. Heard, professor of Materials Science and Engineering at Carnegie Mellon University. He helped us calculate the potential amount of energy, in the form of heat, that ends up in each machine's insert to cook the food, based on the dimensions of each machine's base and insert, and its wattage (power).

Unsurprisingly, the Instant Pot had the least amount of energy reaching the food: 0.19 watts per cubic centimeter, compared to 0.21 to 0.23 watts per cubic centimeter in the other models. Even the Crock-Pot, which cooks at a lower temperature than the Instant Pot, had 0.23 watts per cubic centimeter reaching the food when we used it on the high slow setting (for more information on when to use the low setting and high setting when slow cooking, see page 14). While seemingly minuscule, these differences mean the Instant Pot had 7.6 to 18.5 percent less available energy to cook with, compared to the other models. No wonder it ran slower.

The Best Multicooker on the Market

After weeks of testing, we found that, overall, we liked these machines. They aren't as good as the individual products they promise to replace; a stovetop pressure cooker will cook faster (though these electric models are more hands-off, so this point is debatable), a skillet is still quicker and easier to work in, a slow cooker will cook your food more gently and evenly, and a rice cooker or a stovetop rice-cooking method will give you more discrete grains. But if you want just one machine to do all of the above, a multicooker is a good option—if you buy the right one.

The best model we tested is the Fagor LUX LCD Multicooker ($199.95), though we also like the slightly less-expensive Fagor LUX Multicooker ($169.95). They produce the same results with food, but the LCD version has a few really useful features. First, an alarm sounds when the lid isn't fully sealed. All of the multicookers we tested have silicone gaskets in their lids that facilitate the seal, but sometimes they can fall out of place, which prevents the lid from sealing properly. Without an alarm, the multicooker will just forge ahead and try to build pressure. Typically you notice something's wrong when steam just keeps shooting out the side of the lid and the machine fails to indicate that the target pressure's been reached within the typical time frame, about 20 minutes. You have to start the cooking time over, but the food has already been heated for several minutes, so it can turn out overcooked. The Fagor LUX LCD's alarm solves that problem; if the lid isn't sealed properly, the pot tells you at the outset.

Two other features we like: Its clean LCD interface is easy to operate and tells you very clearly what it's doing, whether it's preheating, cooking under pressure, warming, finished cooking, or doing something else. You also can lock the controls, so you can't accidentally bump them and cancel or change your settings. We think these enhancements are worth $30 more, though the LUX is still a good option.

Finally, for any Instant Pot fanatics reading this, please, put down your pitchforks! While we do think other models are superior because they slow cook in a more timely fashion, which makes them more truly multipurpose, if the Instant Pot works for you, if it makes your life easier, if it motivates you to prepare food more often at home, then it's worth every penny you spent on it.

TESTING MULTICOOKERS

We tested six multicookers priced from $79.99 to $199.95. We made Easy Beef Stew, Braised Chicken Breasts with Tomatoes and Capers, and Boston Baked Beans twice in each machine, first using the pressure cook function and then the slow cook function. We also made white and brown rice. We tracked the multicookers' temperatures on the slow setting on both low and high over 5 hours. We also brought the multicookers up to low and high pressure and tracked their temperatures to see how much pressure they were capable of producing. Products appear below in order of preference.

recommended	performance	comments
 **Fagor** LUX LCD Multicooker **MODEL** 935010063 **SIZE** 8 quart **PRICE** $199.95 **ASIN** B06XCR2BNT **PRESSURE COOKER MAX, LOW** 233.8°, 7.6 psi **PRESSURE COOKER MAX, HIGH** 238.0°, 9.4 psi **SLOW COOKER MAX, LOW** 203.8° **SLOW COOKER MAX, HIGH** 213.1°	PRESSURE COOKING ★★★ SLOW COOKING ★★ RICE COOKING ★★★ SEARING/SAUTÉING ★★★ EASE OF USE ★★★ MANEUVERABILITY ★★★	This model has a couple of features that we really liked. The pressure cooked food was quite good, and the slow cooking function worked fairly well. We liked its clearly labeled lid, which helped us latch it quickly and accurately (unlike the confusing lids of other models), and its LCD interface, which was easy to use and always told us clearly what the cooker was doing. We also appreciated the sensor that alerts you when the lid isn't properly sealed. Lastly, we liked that you can lock the control panel, so you can't accidentally cancel or adjust the settings.
 **Fagor** LUX Multicooker **MODEL** 670041960 **SIZE** 8 quart **PRICE** $169.95 **ASIN** B00ULHPXYA **PRESSURE COOKER MAX, LOW** 235.9°, 8.5 psi **PRESSURE COOKER MAX, HIGH** 240.6°, 10.5 psi **SLOW COOKER MAX, LOW** 200.1° **SLOW COOKER MAX, HIGH** 213.9°	PRESSURE COOKING ★★★ SLOW COOKING ★★ RICE COOKING ★★★ SEARING/SAUTÉING ★★★ EASE OF USE ★★½ MANEUVERABILITY ★★★	This model made great pressure cooked food. And though, like other models, it tended to cook less efficiently than a traditional slow cooker because of its shape, we were able to get good results. It had a comparatively simple and navigable interface, and we really liked the clear "locked" and "unlocked" symbols, which made it easier to attach the lid. It has a lot of buttons, and its interface isn't quite as streamlined as our winner, but it's still a good option.
GoWISE USA 8-Quart 10-in-1 Electric Pressure Cooker / Slow Cooker **BEST BUY** **MODEL** GS22623 **SIZE** 8 quart **PRICE** $89.95 **ASIN** B013TBYQ5Q **PRESSURE COOKER MAX, LOW** 235.2°, 8.3 psi **PRESSURE COOKER MAX, HIGH** 240.4°, 10.5 psi **SLOW COOKER MAX, LOW** 198.0° **SLOW COOKER MAX, HIGH** 214.1°	PRESSURE COOKING ★★★ SLOW COOKING ★★ RICE COOKING ★★★ SEARING/SAUTÉING ★★★ EASE OF USE ★★ MANEUVERABILITY ★★★	This multicooker had a ripping-hot sauté function that browned meat nicely. The unit also worked great as a pressure cooker. It ran a bit hotter than a traditional slow cooker, but overall it made good food. Its interface was a little confusing; it tells you the psi reading but not the temperature, which is not terribly useful unless you're well versed in psi and expected levels. Like most models, its control panel was busy, with a ton of vague, superfluous buttons like "poultry" and "meat/stew." Testers also found the "hours" label next to the timer confusing because it was often counting down minutes, which gave us pause.

recommended with reservations	performance	comments

Instant Pot
Duo 7-in-1 Multi-Use
Programmable Pressure Cooker

MODEL DUO80
SIZE 8 quart
PRICE $129.95
**PRESSURE COOKER MAX,
LOW** 234.4°, 7.9 psi
**PRESSURE COOKER MAX,
HIGH** 246.5°, 13.4 psi
SLOW COOKER MAX, LOW 186.7°
SLOW COOKER MAX, HIGH
206.2°

PRESSURE COOKING ★★★
SLOW COOKING ★
RICE COOKING ★★★
SEARING/SAUTÉING ★★★
EASE OF USE ★★½
MANEUVERABILITY ★★

This machine did a good job pressure cooking, making rice, and searing, but its slow cooking function was extremely slow. Small-volume recipes, thinner soups, or more delicate cuts of meat were fine, but many thick, large-volume recipes like stews and roasts took an insane amount of time: After 11 hours of cooking beef stew on high, the meat was still chewy and the vegetables raw. Even when we used the "high" setting for slow cooked recipes, they still took a very long time. This model ran a little hotter than others under pressure, but this didn't affect most recipes. Lastly, its operating instructions were a bit confusing, and the metal parts on its lid got really hot.

Crock-Pot
Express Crock Multi-Cooker

MODEL SCCPPC600-V1
SIZE 6 quart
PRICE $79.99
**PRESSURE COOKER MAX,
LOW** 228.5°, 5.5 psi
**PRESSURE COOKER MAX,
HIGH** 235.0°, 8.1 psi
SLOW COOKER MAX, LOW 172.0°
SLOW COOKER MAX, HIGH 197.0°

PRESSURE COOKING ★★★
SLOW COOKING ★
RICE COOKING ★★★
SEARING/SAUTÉING ★★★
EASE OF USE ★★
MANEUVERABILITY ★½

This smaller multicooker pressure cooked well, though it took a bit longer than other models to slow cook. Testers also found it more confusing to program: It didn't have a manual mode for pressure cooking, so we always had to select one of the preset buttons (labeled "meat," "chicken," etc.) and adjust the preprogrammed time and temperature as necessary. The insert sat flush with the base and so it was harder to remove, and it had a dark nonstick finish that made monitoring browning difficult. Another drawback: It comes in only a 6-quart size (we preferred 8-quart models because they were larger and thus we could maneuver food more easily in them).

not recommended	performance	comments

Aobosi
Electric Pressure Cooker

MODEL YBW80-120G
SIZE 8 quart
PRICE $88.79
**PRESSURE COOKER MAX,
LOW** 234.8°, 8.0 psi
**PRESSURE COOKER MAX,
HIGH** 238.3°, 9.6 psi
SLOW COOKER MAX 207.9°
(note: model has only one slow cook setting)

PRESSURE COOKING ★
SLOW COOKING ★★
RICE COOKING ★★★
SEARING/SAUTÉING ★
EASE OF USE ★★
MANEUVERABILITY ★

This multicooker had a faulty, drooping gasket that kept the lid from sealing, preventing it from coming up to pressure. With only one temperature setting for slow cooking, this unit tended to overcook delicate foods such as chicken breasts. Its lid was on a hinge, so it got in our way while we were sautéing. It had only one glacially slow searing temperature and automatically shut off after 20 minutes. Lastly, the control panel was complex, with lots of buttons and symbols and confusing words like "less" and "more," instead of "low" and "high."

PRESSURE COOKING IN YOUR MULTICOOKER

Pressure cooking can seem a bit mysterious, and it's no wonder: Once you lock on the lid, it's impossible to know what's happening in the pot. That's why foolproof, thoroughly tested recipes are a must when cooking this way. But there are a few other things to know before you start pressure cooking in your multicooker.

What's Happening?

Pressure cooking functions on a very simple principle: In a tightly sealed pot, the boiling point of liquid is higher. Normally, water boils and turns to steam at 212 degrees Fahrenheit. In a closed environment, however, the water molecules can't escape, increasing the pressure in the pot. Since more energy is needed for the water to boil, the temperature in the pot increases. We measure this in pounds of pressure per square inch, or psi. On the high pressure setting in a multicooker, the pressure reaches between 8.1 and 13.4 psi, or between 235 and 246.5 degrees Fahrenheit. This means that you are cooking food with steam that's at a temperature up to 34 degrees higher than what's possible in a normal pot, which translates to shorter cooking times.

High Pressure vs. Low Pressure

Most multicookers have two pressure levels: high and low. The exact amount of pressure—and therefore the temperature—for each level varies slightly from model to model (see chart on pages 10–11 for more information). We use high pressure in most recipes since it is the most efficient, but we found low pressure produces slightly better results when cooking foods that need a gentler hand, like Flan (page 170) and Cheesecake (page 172).

Natural Release vs. Quick Release

There are two methods to release pressure after cooking: quick release and natural release. The one you use will affect the final outcome of a recipe—so don't swap one for the other. What's the difference, and why do we use both?

Natural release If you do nothing when the cooking time ends, the multicooker will allow the pressure in the pot to drop back down naturally. This is the preferred method when you want to gently finish cooking food through, since food will continue to cook in the residual heat as the pressure drops. A natural release can also affect texture: If you quickly release the pressure on a large cut of meat like our Classic Pot Roast with Mushroom Gravy, the meat will seize up and be tough. Because the rate at which the pressure releases varies from pot to pot, after 15 minutes we often quick-release any remaining pressure (at this point, depending on the amount of food in the pot, there may or may not be pressure left in the pot). This helps keep the recipe results uniform, no matter the multicooker.

Quick release You can immediately release pressure by turning the pressure regulator knob to "steam" or "venting" as soon as your recipe is done cooking. Be careful—the steam will be hot. We usually use a quick release when we want to stop the cooking right away because the food can easily overcook (think chicken breasts). Or, if a gentle finish isn't important, we simply opt for a quick release because it's faster.

Pressure Cooker Safety

Pressure cooking in a multicooker is safer than ever, with multiple fail-safes in place to prevent explosions and other mishaps. But even though the multicooker is a far cry from your grandmother's pressure cooker, there are still right and wrong ways to use it. Before you start cooking, be sure to read over the points below—these things are of paramount importance to ensure you stay safe and get the best results every time.

DO	DON'T
DO read your multicooker's manual for model-specific recommendations regarding safety and proper use.	DON'T use the food-specific buttons on your multicooker, such as "stew" or "risotto," for our recipes—these are usually just variations on the pressure setting, and they give you less control over the final product. We recommend using our pressure cooking instructions and entering the time yourself.
DO make sure the silicone gasket in the lid is in place and in good shape (soft and springy, not dry or cracked). Remove and clean the gasket after every use.	DON'T use a gasket other than the one that's made specifically to fit your exact brand of multicooker; gaskets are not standardized. You can order replacement gaskets (and other parts) directly from the manufacturer.
DO clean the vents and inspect the valves before and after every use. Make sure the valves aren't clogged, especially after cooking foaming, starchy foods such as rice or beans. If the valves seem sticky or hard to manipulate, consult your manual for cleaning instructions.	DON'T change the type of release called for in the recipe—it will change the results for the worse.
DO read every recipe from beginning to end before you start cooking.	DON'T fill the pot past the maximum fill line (or, two-thirds full for most recipes except for foaming and expanding foods, in which case the pot should be only half full).
DO be sure to add enough liquid for the pot to pressurize. All of the recipes in this book are designed to meet the minimum requirement for pressurizing the pot, often using a combination of liquid added directly to the pot and juices released by the food itself. Check your manual for liquid guidelines if you are creating your own recipes.	DON'T force the cooker open before the pressure has been released.
DO let steam escape away from you when removing the lid after cooking. The steam is extremely hot, so use a towel or oven mitts to protect your hands.	DON'T try to deep-fry food under pressure—the oil will get dangerously hot.

SLOW COOKING IN YOUR MULTICOOKER

Slow cooking in your multicooker is not like slow cooking in a traditional slow cooker: The multicooker heats more rapidly than a slow cooker, though often not as evenly, and the pot can pressurize slightly even though the release valve is left open. As a result, slow cooked recipes tend to cook faster than in traditional slow cookers, so recipes must be tailored for the special environment of the multicooker. Here's what's important to know for slow cooking success in your multicooker.

High Slow vs. Low Slow

Many multicookers—though not all—have a high and a low slow cook setting. For most multicookers with this option, we found that the low setting worked better, since the aim is gentle cooking. The Instant Pot was an exception: The low slow cook setting was actually too low (about 17 degrees lower than our winner). As a result, we always use the high slow cook setting for the Instant Pot, which puts the temperature within our suggested temperature range of 195 to 210 degrees. We also suggest using the high setting for the Crock-Pot, which runs too cool on the low setting.

Using the Time Ranges

Many of the slow cook time ranges in this book are 1-hour ranges to help account for differences in multicooker sizes and cooking temperatures. Start checking for doneness at the beginning of the range to avoid overcooking; once you know how your multicooker cooks, you'll have a better idea of whether you need to cook to the beginning or the end of the range.

SHOULD I USE HIGH OR LOW TO SLOW COOK?

Because each multicooker model runs differently—and the temperatures given in the manuals are not always accurate—getting slow cooked recipes just right may require some trial and error. If you like, you can run a simple test that will tell you the approximate temperature of your multicooker on the slow settings, sidestepping some of the guesswork. You want to aim to slow cook at a temperature between 195 and 210 degrees, so choose high or low based on which setting falls in that range.

To perform the test, fill your multicooker with 4 quarts of room-temperature water (70 degrees). Turn on the low slow setting and let the multicooker run for 1 hour. Using an instant-read thermometer, take the temperature of the water. Repeat with the high slow setting if necessary.

TROUBLESHOOTING IN YOUR MULTICOOKER

The more you use your multicooker, the better your results will be—you'll know more about how your pot cooks, how hot it runs on various settings, and what to keep in mind when using it. But the learning curve can be a challenge if you've never used your cooker, or if you use it only infrequently. Here are a few common problems you may run into while using your multicooker, and how to solve them.

PROBLEM	SOLUTION	NOTES
Undercooked food when using the pressure cook setting	Continue to cook the food using the highest sauté or browning function.	Since it's impossible to test the doneness of food as it cooks under pressure, sometimes food might be slightly underdone. Simply finish cooking by switching to the highest sauté or browning function, adding extra liquid as needed.
Undercooked food when using the slow cook setting	Extend the slow cook time, or switch to the highest sauté or browning function.	Some multicookers run hotter or cooler than others, so if food is not done cooking in the time range specified, replace the lid and continue to check the food periodically. If you're short on time, you can try to speed up the process by switching to the highest sauté or browning function and simmering the food until it's done, though this may require you to add liquid to the pot to prevent scorching.
Uneven cooking	Prep ingredients as directed.	Because the multicooker's heating element is on the bottom of the pot, some foods can cook unevenly. There's no going back on an unevenly cooked dish, but to ensure the best results next time, be sure that your ingredients are prepped properly: Buy the right-size roast or chicken, measure liquids accurately, and grab a ruler when prepping vegetables.
Sauce is too thick, or too thin	Add more liquid, or continue to simmer.	A lot of variables can affect the texture of a sauce, and these include your multicooker's heat level and the freshness of the ingredients. Sauces that are too thin can simply be simmered uncovered on the highest sauté or browning function to thicken up before serving, and thick sauces can be thinned out with additional broth or water.
Scorching during pressure or slow cooking	Add additional liquid and scrape up browned bits.	If you find that food is burning while you're sautéing, try adding a small amount of liquid to slow down the cooking. Although you can't fix food that has been burned during pressure or slow cooking, you can avoid the problem in the future by taking care to scrape up all the browned bits left in the pot after sautéing food and before closing the lid. In addition, be sure there is enough liquid in the pot (we made sure that the recipes in this book contain enough liquid to prevent scorching, but keep an eye out when using your own recipes).
Never reaching pressure	Check your silicone gasket and pressure regulating knob.	If your pot is not coming to pressure, it may not be sealed correctly. Check that the silicone gasket around the bottom lip of the lid is not cracked or improperly installed, and make sure that the pressure regulating knob (found on the lid) is in the closed position.

SOUPS, STEWS, AND CHILIS

CLASSIC CHICKEN NOODLE SOUP

serves 6 to 8

pressure cook total time 1 hour	slow cook total time 3 hours 30 minutes

why this recipe works With its velvety broth and deep, comforting flavor, old-fashioned chicken noodle soup is a perfect candidate for the multicooker: You can't beat the sheer convenience, and the closed environment is ideal for extracting tons of flavor and body-building gelatin from the meat, skin, and bones of a whole chicken, whether through high-heat pressure cooking or long slow cooking. We started by using the sauté function to brown our aromatics; tomato paste and soy sauce boosted the savory flavor of our soup. We found we didn't need to spend time cutting up the chicken—we could put the whole chicken right in the pot. We made sure to place the chicken breast side up: The multicooker heats from the bottom, so positioning the chicken this way exposed the dark meat thighs to more direct heat and shielded the delicate breast meat from overcooking. Once cooked, the tender meat practically fell off the bones, making it easy to shred and stir back in. Rather than lugging out a second pot to cook the noodles, we simply used the sauté function to simmer the noodles right in the broth. We prefer to use wide egg noodles in this soup, but thin egg noodles can be substituted; thin egg noodles will have a shorter cooking time in step 4. Cook the noodles just before serving to keep them from overcooking and turning mushy.

1 tablespoon vegetable oil

1 onion, chopped fine

Salt and pepper

1 tablespoon tomato paste

3 garlic cloves, minced

2 teaspoons minced fresh thyme or ½ teaspoon dried

8 cups water

4 carrots, peeled, halved lengthwise, and sliced ½ inch thick

2 celery ribs, sliced ½ inch thick

2 tablespoons soy sauce

1 (4-pound) whole chicken, giblets discarded

4 ounces (2 cups) wide egg noodles

¼ cup minced fresh parsley

1 Using highest sauté or browning function, heat oil in multicooker until shimmering. Add onion and ½ teaspoon salt and cook until onion is softened, 3 to 5 minutes. Stir in tomato paste, garlic, and thyme and cook until fragrant, about 30 seconds. Stir in 6 cups water, carrots, celery, and soy sauce, scraping up any browned bits. Season chicken with salt and pepper and place breast side up in multicooker.

2A to pressure cook Lock lid in place and close pressure release valve. Select high pressure cook function and cook for 20 minutes. Turn off multicooker and quick-release pressure. Carefully remove lid, allowing steam to escape away from you.

2B to slow cook Lock lid in place and open pressure release valve. Select low slow cook function and cook until chicken is tender, 2 to 3 hours. (If using Instant Pot, select high slow cook function.) Carefully remove lid, allowing steam to escape away from you.

3 Transfer chicken to cutting board, let cool slightly, then shred into bite-size pieces using 2 forks; discard skin and bones.

4 Meanwhile, stir remaining 2 cups water into soup. If necessary, cook using highest sauté or browning function until vegetables are just tender, 5 to 10 minutes. Stir in noodles

and cook until tender, about 8 minutes. Turn off multi-cooker. Stir in chicken and let sit until heated through, about 2 minutes. Stir in parsley and season with salt and pepper to taste. Serve.

CLASSIC CHICKEN NOODLE SOUP WITH ORZO, GREEN BEANS, AND PEAS

Substitute 1 leek, white and light green parts only, quartered lengthwise, sliced thin, and washed thoroughly, for onion; ¾ cup orzo for egg noodles; and 2 tablespoons minced fresh tarragon for parsley. Stir 8 ounces green beans, trimmed and cut into 1-inch lengths, into soup with orzo. Stir ½ cup thawed frozen peas into soup with shredded chicken.

CLASSIC CHICKEN NOODLE SOUP WITH SHELLS, TOMATOES, AND ZUCCHINI

Substitute 1 cup small pasta shells for egg noodles, and chopped fresh basil for parsley. Stir 1 chopped tomato and 1 zucchini, cut into ½-inch pieces, into soup with pasta.

TORTILLA SOUP

serves 6 to 8

pressure cook total time 50 minutes	slow cook total time 3 hours 30 minutes

why this recipe works This light yet deeply flavorful soup is a celebration of colors, tastes, and textures, overflowing with garnishes and tender shredded chicken. We wanted it to have authentic flavor with a streamlined method, and the multicooker was the perfect ally. To replicate the traditionally deep, roasty, smoky notes of the broth, typically achieved by charring the vegetables, we used the sauté function to brown some of the vegetables and aromatics. Using chipotle chile in adobo sauce (which are dried, smoked jalapeños in a spicy chile sauce) also added some smokiness along with a spicy kick, and a bit of tomato paste gave the base deep, savory flavor. Since the tortillas are an essential component of the soup, we decided to add some tortilla pieces right to the pot to give the soup better body; the tortillas softened during cooking, and a vigorous whisk at the end ensured the pieces broke down. Since the base already had so much flavor, we found that making our own broth wasn't necessary, so we used store-bought broth and quicker-cooking boneless chicken; tasters preferred thighs over breasts for their richer flavor. Since the multicooker gave the soup great long-cooked flavor, we amped up the freshness and spice by stirring in additional aromatics after cooking. The tortilla strips are best prepared the day of serving. Different brands of corn tortillas may vary in thickness; the cooking time for the tortilla strips may need to be adjusted based on how thick yours are. Don't skip the garnishes—they are an essential component of the dish. If you can't find Cotija cheese, substitute farmer's cheese or feta.

2 tablespoons vegetable oil

2 tomatoes, cored and chopped

1 onion, chopped fine

2 jalapeño chiles, stemmed, seeded, and minced

6 garlic cloves, minced

1 tablespoon minced canned chipotle chile in adobo sauce

1 tablespoon tomato paste

6 cups chicken broth

10 (6-inch) corn tortillas (4 cut into ½-inch pieces, 6 halved and cut crosswise into ½-inch wide strips)

1½ pounds boneless, skinless chicken thighs, trimmed

Salt and pepper

8 ounces Cotija cheese, crumbled (2 cups)

1 avocado, halved, pitted, and cut into ½-inch pieces

½ cup sour cream

½ cup minced fresh cilantro

Lime wedges

1 Using highest sauté or browning function, heat 1 tablespoon oil in multicooker until shimmering. Add tomatoes, onion, and half of jalapeños and cook until softened, about 5 to 7 minutes. Stir in garlic, 2 teaspoons chipotle, and tomato paste and cook until fragrant, about 1 minute. Stir in broth and tortilla pieces, scraping up any browned bits. Season chicken with salt and pepper and nestle into multicooker.

2A to pressure cook Lock lid in place and close pressure release valve. Select high pressure cook function and cook for 5 minutes. Turn off multicooker and quick-release pressure. Carefully remove lid, allowing steam to escape away from you.

2B to slow cook Lock lid in place and open pressure release valve. Select low slow cook function and cook until chicken is tender, 2 to 3 hours. (If using Instant Pot, select high slow cook function.) Turn off multicooker and carefully remove lid, allowing steam to escape away from you.

3 Meanwhile, adjust oven rack to middle position and heat oven to 425 degrees. Toss tortilla strips with remaining 1 tablespoon oil and bake on rimmed baking sheet until crisp and deep golden, 8 to 12 minutes, stirring occasionally. Transfer strips to paper towel–lined plate and lightly season with salt to taste; set aside for serving.

4 Transfer chicken to cutting board, let cool slightly, then shred into bite-size pieces using 2 forks. Whisk soup vigorously for 30 seconds to break down tortilla pieces. Stir in chicken, remaining jalapeños, and remaining 1 teaspoon chipotle and let sit until heated through, about 2 minutes. Season with salt and pepper to taste. Serve, passing toasted tortilla strips, Cotija, avocado, sour cream, cilantro, and lime wedges separately.

SPICY MOROCCAN-STYLE CHICKEN AND LENTIL SOUP

serves 8

pressure cook total time 55 minutes	slow cook total time 2 hours 30 minutes

why this recipe works For this unique chicken soup, we took inspiration from Moroccan *harira*, an intensely flavored soup made with lentils, tomatoes, and chicken. Since traditional recipes often call for a laundry list of hard-to-find ingredients, we simplified with a careful selection of accessible, impactful flavor builders. Bone-in split chicken breasts offered rich flavor; after browning them, we bloomed a fragrant combination of fresh ginger and warm spices. Flour provided some thickening power. Whether we pressure or slow cooked it, the chicken turned out perfectly tender, ready to be shredded and stirred back into the soup. Plum tomatoes, cut into large pieces, added traditional tomato flavor and freshness. Harissa, a spicy paste of chiles, spices, garlic, and olive oil, was a delicious finishing touch to this Moroccan-style recipe. Large green or brown lentils work well in this recipe; do not use French green lentils (*lentilles du puy*).

1½ pounds bone-in split chicken breasts, trimmed

Salt and pepper

1 tablespoon extra-virgin olive oil

1 tablespoon all-purpose flour

1 teaspoon grated fresh ginger

1 teaspoon ground cumin

½ teaspoon paprika

¼ teaspoon ground cinnamon

¼ teaspoon cayenne pepper

Pinch saffron threads, crumbled

10 cups chicken broth

1 cup brown or green lentils, picked over and rinsed

4 plum tomatoes, cored and cut into ¾-inch pieces

⅓ cup minced fresh cilantro

¼ cup harissa, plus extra for serving

1 Pat chicken dry with paper towels and season with salt and pepper. Using highest sauté or browning function, heat oil in multicooker for 5 minutes (or until just smoking). Brown chicken, 3 to 5 minutes per side; transfer to plate.

2 Add flour, ginger, cumin, paprika, cinnamon, cayenne, ¼ teaspoon pepper, and saffron to fat left in multicooker and cook until fragrant, about 1 minute. Slowly whisk in broth, scraping up any browned bits and smoothing out any lumps. Stir in lentils, then nestle chicken, skin side up, into multicooker, adding any accumulated juices.

3A to pressure cook Lock lid in place and close pressure release valve. Select high pressure cook function and cook for 8 minutes. Turn off multicooker and quick-release pressure. Carefully remove lid, allowing steam to escape away from you.

3B to slow cook Lock lid in place and open pressure release valve. Select low slow cook function and cook until chicken is tender, 1 to 2 hours. (If using Instant Pot, select high slow cook function.) Turn off multicooker and carefully remove lid, allowing steam to escape away from you.

4 Transfer chicken to cutting board, let cool slightly, then shred into bite-size pieces using 2 forks; discard skin and bones.

5 If lentils are still firm, continue to cook lentils using highest sauté or browning function until lentils are just tender, about 5 minutes. Turn off multicooker. Stir in chicken and tomatoes and let sit until heated through, about 2 minutes. Stir in cilantro and harissa and season with salt and pepper to taste. Serve, passing extra harissa separately.

EASY BEEF AND BARLEY SOUP

serves 6 to 8

| pressure cook total time 1 hour | slow cook total time 4 hours 30 minutes |

why this recipe works Beef and barley soup should be packed with tender beef and nicely al dente grains. The key to making this soup in the multicooker was getting the beef and the barley to cook in the same amount of time. We started by trading in the traditional large roast for smaller blade steaks. These steaks are nicely marbled and have great beefy flavor, but since they are considerably smaller and thinner than a roast, they cooked to perfect tenderness at the same rate as the barley. Even better, we didn't need to spend time browning the steaks; we could simply brown the mushrooms and aromatics for a deeply flavored base. A generous amount of soy sauce helped to boost savory flavor, while the classic additions of celery and carrots, cut into ½-inch pieces so they would cook in the same amount of time as the rest of the soup ingredients, gave the soup some extra flavor. Since pearl barley can absorb quite a bit of liquid, we needed to be judicious in the amount we added to the soup. A modest ½ cup lent the soup a velvety texture without turning it into a thick stew. Do not substitute hulled, hull-less, quick-cooking, or presteamed barley (read the ingredient list on the package to determine this) in this recipe.

1 tablespoon vegetable oil

8 ounces cremini mushrooms, trimmed and sliced ½ inch thick

1 onion, chopped fine

2 celery ribs, cut into ½-inch pieces

Salt and pepper

2 tablespoons all-purpose flour

2 tablespoons tomato paste

2 teaspoons minced fresh thyme or ½ teaspoon dried

6 cups beef broth

2 tablespoons soy sauce

3 carrots, peeled and cut into ½-inch pieces

½ cup pearl barley

1 pound boneless beef blade steaks, trimmed and cut into ½-inch pieces

2 tablespoons minced fresh parsley

1 Using highest sauté or browning function, heat oil in multicooker until shimmering. Add mushrooms, onion, celery, and ½ teaspoon salt and cook until vegetables are softened, 6 to 8 minutes. Stir in flour, tomato paste, and thyme and cook until fragrant, about 1 minute. Slowly whisk in broth, soy sauce, carrots, and barley, scraping up any browned bits and smoothing out any lumps. Season beef with salt and pepper and stir into multicooker.

2A to pressure cook Lock lid in place and close pressure release valve. Select high pressure cook function and cook for 20 minutes. Turn off multicooker and quick-release pressure. Carefully remove lid, allowing steam to escape away from you.

2B to slow cook Lock lid in place and open pressure release valve. Select low slow cook function and cook until beef is tender, 3 to 4 hours. (If using Instant Pot, select high slow cook function and increase cooking range to 4 to 5 hours.) Turn off multicooker and carefully remove lid, allowing steam to escape away from you.

3 Stir in parsley and season with salt and pepper to taste. Serve.

VIETNAMESE BEEF PHO

serves 4 to 6

| pressure cook total time 2 hours 45 minutes | slow cook total time 9 hours 45 minutes |

why this recipe works With its richly perfumed broth and its mix of raw/cooked and hot/cold ingredients, this Vietnamese soup is a delicious study in contrasts. Arguably the most important element is the beefy, fragrant, faintly sweet broth produced by simmering beef bones with aromatics such as ginger, onions, cinnamon, and star anise. The multicooker was a perfect vessel for this recipe, whether we used the high heat of the pressure cooker or the low, even heat of the slow cooker. However we chose to cook our broth, we found that a relatively long cooking time was needed to fully extract all of the beefy flavor from the bones. To amp up the savoriness and depth of the broth, we browned the bones in the microwave before cooking (the large, unevenly shaped bones were too difficult to brown in the narrow multicooker insert). To further boost beefy flavor, we added the trimmings from the steaks we were slicing for the finished soup. To give our deeply aromatic broth the clean, clear look that is a hallmark of pho, we strained and defatted it after cooking. The rest of the soup components were simple: We soaked rice noodles to soften them, then finished cooking them right in the broth so they would pick up more flavor. We thinly sliced the steaks (freezing them briefly made them firm enough to slice easily) and ladled the hot broth over the slices, which cooked them just enough. We topped the bowls with traditional garnishes like thinly sliced onion, bean sprouts, cilantro, and fish sauce. An equal weight of tri-tip steak or blade steak can be substituted for the strip steak; make sure to trim all connective tissue and excess fat. Look for noodles that are about ⅛ inch wide; these are often labeled "small." Don't use Thai Kitchen Stir-Fry Rice Noodles; they are too thick and don't adequately soak up the broth.

3 pounds beef bones	6 whole cloves	⅓ cup chopped fresh cilantro
2 onions, quartered through root end	Salt	3 scallions, sliced thin (optional)
3 quarts water	1 teaspoon black peppercorns	Bean sprouts
¼ cup fish sauce, plus extra for serving	1 (1-pound) boneless strip steak, 1½ to 1¾ inches thick, trimmed and halved crosswise, trimmings reserved	Fresh Thai or Italian basil sprigs
1 (4-inch) piece ginger, peeled and sliced into ⅛-inch-thick rounds		Lime wedges
1 cinnamon stick	14–16 ounces (⅛-inch-wide) rice noodles	Hoisin sauce
6 star anise pods		Sriracha sauce

1 Arrange beef bones on paper towel–lined plate and microwave (in batches, if microwave is small) until well browned, 8 to 10 minutes. Add bones and 6 onion quarters to multicooker. Slice remaining 2 onion quarters as thin as possible and set aside for serving. Add 2 quarts water, fish sauce, ginger, cinnamon stick, star anise, cloves, 1 tablespoon salt, peppercorns, and reserved steak trimmings to multicooker.

2A **to pressure cook** Lock lid in place and close pressure release valve. Select high pressure cook function and cook for 1½ hours. Turn off multicooker and let pressure release naturally for 15 minutes. Quick-release any remaining pressure, then carefully remove lid, allowing steam to escape away from you.

2B to slow cook Lock lid in place and open pressure release valve. Select low slow cook function and cook until broth is deeply flavored, 8 to 9 hours. (If using Instant Pot, select high slow cook function.) Turn off multicooker and carefully remove lid, allowing steam to escape away from you.

3 Discard bones. Strain broth through fine-mesh strainer into clean container, pressing on solids to extract as much liquid as possible; discard solids. Let broth settle, then skim excess fat from surface using large spoon. Return broth and remaining 1 quart water to multicooker and season with salt to taste (broth should taste overseasoned).

4 Meanwhile, place steak on large plate and freeze until very firm, 35 to 45 minutes. Once firm, cut against grain into ⅛-inch-thick slices. Return steak to plate and refrigerate until needed.

5 Place noodles in large container and cover with hot tap water. Soak until noodles are pliable, 10 to 15 minutes; drain noodles.

6 Bring broth to boil using highest sauté or browning function. Add noodles and cook until softened, about 90 seconds. Turn off multicooker. Using tongs, divide noodles between individual serving bowls. Divide steak among bowls, shingling slices on top of noodles. Pile reserved onion slices on top of steak slices and sprinkle with cilantro and scallions, if using. Ladle hot broth into each bowl. Serve immediately, passing bean sprouts, basil sprigs, lime wedges, hoisin, Sriracha, and extra fish sauce separately.

SICILIAN CHICKPEA AND ESCAROLE SOUP

serves 6 to 8

pressure cook total time	slow cook total time
50 minutes (plus brining time)	5 hours 30 minutes (plus brining time)

why this recipe works Dried chickpeas have a beautifully creamy, soft texture when cooked, and the multicooker is a great way to get them evenly cooked either under pressure or by slow cooking. We opted to develop a Sicilian-style soup that paired these mild beans with bright, slightly bitter escarole. Brining the chickpeas ensured fewer blowouts and tender beans. Some classic Sicilian flavors, like fennel, garlic, and oregano, gave the soup an aromatic profile. A Parmesan rind bolstered the broth with richness and complexity. To keep the escarole fresh-tasting and crunchy, we waited to add it until after pressure or slow cooking. A fresh tomato, stirred in with the escarole, offered some bright acidity. You'll get fewer blowouts if you soak the chickpeas overnight, but if you're pressed for time, you can quick-salt-soak your chickpeas: In step 1, combine the salt, water, and chickpeas in the multicooker and bring them to a boil using the highest sauté or browning function. Turn off the multicooker, cover, and let the chickpeas sit for 1 hour. Drain and rinse the chickpeas and proceed with the recipe as directed.

Salt and pepper

1 pound (2¾ cups) dried chickpeas, picked over and rinsed

1 tablespoon extra-virgin olive oil, plus extra for drizzling

2 fennel bulbs, stalks discarded, bulbs halved, cored, and chopped fine

5 garlic cloves, minced

2 teaspoons minced fresh oregano or ½ teaspoon dried

¼ teaspoon red pepper flakes

4 cups chicken or vegetable broth

1 Parmesan cheese rind (optional), plus grated Parmesan for serving

2 bay leaves

½ head escarole (8 ounces), trimmed and cut into 1-inch pieces

1 large tomato, cored and chopped

1 Dissolve 3 tablespoons salt in 4 quarts cold water in large container. Add chickpeas and soak at room temperature for at least 8 hours or up to 24 hours. Drain and rinse well.

2 Using highest sauté or browning function, heat 1 tablespoon oil in multicooker until shimmering. Add fennel and ½ teaspoon salt and cook until fennel is softened, 5 to 7 minutes. Stir in garlic, oregano, and pepper flakes and cook until fragrant, about 30 seconds. Stir in 3 cups water, broth, Parmesan rind (if using), bay leaves, and chickpeas.

3A to pressure cook Lock lid in place and close pressure release valve. Select high pressure cook function and cook for 12 minutes. Turn off multicooker and quick-release pressure. Carefully remove lid, allowing steam to escape away from you.

3B to slow cook Lock lid in place and open pressure release valve. Select low slow cook function and cook until chickpeas are tender, 4 to 5 hours. (If using Instant Pot, select high slow cook function.) Carefully remove lid, allowing steam to escape away from you.

4 Discard bay leaves and Parmesan rind, if using. Stir in escarole, 1 handful at a time, and tomato and cook using highest sauté or browning function until escarole is wilted, about 5 minutes. Turn off multicooker. Season with salt and pepper to taste. Drizzle individual portions with extra oil and serve, passing Parmesan separately.

WILD RICE SOUP WITH COCONUT AND LIME

serves 6 to 8

pressure cook total time 1 hour	slow cook total time 3 hours 30 minutes

why this recipe works We set out to make a light and fresh coconut soup featuring tender wild rice and earthy mushrooms. We tried putting all of the broth ingredients in the pot with the wild rice from the start, but found that the flavor became too dull after cooking. To make sure our soup turned out bright, we reserved half of the coconut milk, along with Thai red curry paste and lime juice, to stir in after pressure or slow cooking. Likewise, we stirred the mushrooms in with the coconut milk mixture toward the end to ensure that the soup's flavor didn't become muddy. We preferred a combination of mushrooms, but 12 ounces of any one type will work. Do not use quick-cooking or presteamed wild rice (read the ingredient list on the package to determine this) in this recipe.

2 tablespoons vegetable oil

2 onions, chopped fine

6 garlic cloves, minced

2 tablespoons grated fresh ginger

4 cups chicken broth

2 (14-ounce) cans coconut milk

1 cup wild rice, picked over and rinsed

2 lemon grass stalks, trimmed to bottom 6 inches and bruised with back of knife

3 tablespoons fish sauce, plus extra for seasoning

4 sprigs fresh cilantro, plus leaves for serving

3 tablespoons lime juice (2 limes), plus lime wedges for serving

1 tablespoon sugar

1 tablespoon Thai red curry paste

12 ounces cremini, shiitake, or white mushrooms, trimmed and sliced thin

Salt and pepper

2 scallions, sliced thin

1 Using highest sauté or browning function, heat oil in multi-cooker until shimmering. Add onions and cook until softened, 3 to 5 minutes. Stir in garlic and ginger and cook until fragrant, about 30 seconds. Stir in broth, 1 can coconut milk, rice, lemon grass, 1 tablespoon fish sauce, and cilantro sprigs.

2A **to pressure cook** Lock lid in place and close pressure release valve. Select high pressure cook function and cook for 23 minutes. Turn off multicooker and quick-release pressure. Carefully remove lid, allowing steam to escape away from you.

2B **to slow cook** Lock lid in place and open pressure release valve. Select low slow cook function and cook until rice is tender, 2 to 3 hours. (If using Instant Pot, select high slow cook function.) Carefully remove lid, allowing steam to escape away from you.

3 Discard lemon grass and cilantro sprigs. Whisk remaining 1 can coconut milk, remaining 2 tablespoons fish sauce, lime juice, sugar, and curry paste together in bowl. Stir coconut milk mixture and mushrooms into soup and cook using highest sauté or browning function until mushrooms are just tender, 3 to 5 minutes. Turn off multicooker. Season with extra fish sauce and salt and pepper to taste. Top individual portions with cilantro leaves and scallions and serve, passing lime wedges separately.

EASY BEEF STEW

serves 4 to 6

why this recipe works We wanted a beef stew that we could make on a weeknight—one that would be mostly hands-off but would still produce tender meat and a thick, luxurious gravy. We started with a beefy chuck-eye roast. The moist heat effortlessly tenderized the tough cut, and we found we could skip the time-consuming browning of the beef by sautéing our aromatics to create plenty of fond and adding a hefty amount of savory soy sauce and tomato paste. Flour helped thicken the stew to give it good body. To keep the potatoes and carrots tender but distinct through cooking, we cut them into large 1-inch pieces. Peas are a classic addition to beef stew, but the intense pressure or extended cooking would cause them to disintegrate; instead, we simply stirred them into the hot stew after cooking so they could warm through. If using an Instant Pot, do not choose the slow cook function; the beef and vegetables will not cook through properly.

1 tablespoon vegetable oil

1 onion, chopped fine

Salt and pepper

¼ cup all-purpose flour

¼ cup tomato paste

1 teaspoon minced fresh thyme or ¼ teaspoon dried

2 cups beef broth, plus extra as needed

2 tablespoons soy sauce

2 pounds boneless beef chuck-eye roast, pulled apart at seams, trimmed, and cut into 1-inch pieces

1 pound red potatoes, unpeeled, cut into 1-inch pieces

1 pound carrots, peeled and sliced 1 inch thick

2 cups frozen peas, thawed

2 tablespoons minced fresh parsley

1 Using highest sauté or browning function, heat oil in multicooker until shimmering. Add onion and ½ teaspoon salt and cook until onion is softened, 3 to 5 minutes. Stir in flour, tomato paste, and thyme and cook until fragrant, about 1 minute. Slowly whisk in broth and soy sauce, scraping up any browned bits and smoothing out any lumps. Season beef with salt and pepper and stir into multicooker along with potatoes and carrots.

2A to pressure cook Lock lid in place and close pressure release valve. Select high pressure cook function and cook for 25 minutes. Turn off multicooker and quick-release pressure. Carefully remove lid, allowing steam to escape away from you.

2B to slow cook (Do not use Instant Pot to slow cook this recipe.) Lock lid in place and open pressure release valve. Select low slow cook function and cook until beef is tender, 7 to 8 hours. Turn off multicooker and carefully remove lid, allowing steam to escape away from you.

3 Stir in peas and let sit until heated through, about 2 minutes. Adjust consistency with extra hot broth as needed. Stir in parsley and season with salt and pepper to taste. Serve.

EASY BEEF STEW WITH BACON AND MUSHROOMS

Omit potatoes and peas. Using highest sauté or browning function, cook 5 slices chopped bacon until browned and crisp, 5 to 7 minutes. Using slotted spoon, transfer bacon to bowl; set aside. Substitute bacon fat left in multicooker for oil in step 1. Add 1 pound quartered white mushrooms to multicooker with onion and cook until vegetables are softened and lightly browned, 10 to 12 minutes; continue with recipe as directed. Stir reserved bacon into stew with parsley.

EASY BEEF STEW WITH TOMATOES, OLIVES, AND ORANGE ZEST

Omit carrots. Add 1 (2-inch) strip orange zest to multi-cooker with flour. Substitute 2 teaspoons herbes de Provence for thyme, two 15-ounce cans chopped tomatoes, drained, for carrots, and 1 cup pitted and halved kalamata olives for peas. Discard zest before serving.

TUSCAN BEEF STEW

serves 6 to 8

| pressure cook total time 1 hour 10 minutes | slow cook total time 8 hours 40 minutes |

why this recipe works Tuscan beef stew is a surprisingly elegant dish of beef braised in Chianti wine. To ensure a rich-tasting, company-worthy result, we chose silky, fall-apart boneless short ribs for their tender texture. Tasters loved the deep flavor of the stew when we browned the ribs; we found we could brown just half the meat to achieve great savory depth. While traditionally this stew is braised in just Chianti wine, the wine wasn't able to reduce and evaporate enough in the enclosed multicooker, making the final stew taste too harsh and acidic. To solve this, we used just a cup of Chianti and supplemented it with rich beef broth. Tomato paste, anchovy, and rosemary, along with the traditional garlic and black pepper, further mellowed the wine's acidity and produced a stew with rounded, balanced flavor. Straying from tradition, we also added pearl onions for some contrasting sweetness. Frozen pearl onions, browned in the rendered beef fat with the rest of the aromatics, held up well in the multicooker. If you cannot find boneless short ribs, substitute 5 pounds of boneless chuck-eye roast. If Chianti is unavailable, a medium-bodied wine such as Côtes du Rhône or Pinot Noir makes a nice substitute. If using an Instant Pot, do not choose the slow cook function; the beef and vegetables will not cook through properly.

3 pounds boneless short ribs, trimmed and cut into 1-inch pieces

Salt and pepper

2 tablespoons extra-virgin olive oil

2½ cups frozen pearl onions, thawed and patted dry

⅓ cup all-purpose flour

4 garlic cloves, sliced thin

1 tablespoon tomato paste

2 teaspoons minced fresh rosemary or ½ teaspoon dried

1 anchovy fillet, rinsed and minced

1 cup Chianti

1¼ cups beef broth, plus extra as needed

2 tablespoons minced fresh parsley

1 Pat beef dry with paper towels and season with salt and pepper. Using highest sauté or browning function, heat 1 tablespoon oil in multicooker for 5 minutes (or until just smoking). Brown half of beef on all sides, 8 to 10 minutes; transfer to bowl. Set aside remaining uncooked beef.

2 Add onions, 2 teaspoons pepper, ½ teaspoon salt, and remaining 1 tablespoon oil to now-empty multicooker and cook until onion is softened, 3 to 5 minutes. Stir in flour, garlic, tomato paste, rosemary, and anchovy and cook until fragrant, about 1 minute. Slowly whisk in Chianti, scraping up any browned bits and smoothing out any lumps. Stir in broth, browned beef and any accumulated juices, and remaining uncooked beef.

3A to pressure cook Lock lid in place and close pressure release valve. Select high pressure cook function and cook for 25 minutes. Turn off multicooker and quick-release pressure. Carefully remove lid, allowing steam to escape away from you.

3B to slow cook (Do not use Instant Pot to slow cook this recipe.) Lock lid in place and open pressure release valve. Select low slow cook function and cook until beef is tender, 7 to 8 hours. Turn off multicooker and carefully remove lid, allowing steam to escape away from you.

4 Using large spoon, skim excess fat from surface of stew. Adjust consistency with extra hot broth as needed. Stir in parsley and season with salt and pepper to taste. Serve.

CHIPOTLE PORK AND HOMINY STEW

serves 6 to 8

pressure cook total time 1 hour 10 minutes   slow cook total time 5 hours 40 minutes

why this recipe works Also known as *posole*, this fragrant and spicy New Mexican stew combines toothsome hominy and tender chunks of pork in a mildly spicy, verdant base. We wanted to use the multicooker to make a streamlined version that would maintain the stew's characteristically complex flavor. Plenty of onion plus jalapeños and garlic offered a bold base, while a bit of chipotle chile in adobo brought smoky depth and spice. In the insulated heat of the multicooker, the pork cooked up ultratender. We also found that adding canned hominy before pressure or slow cooking allowed it to soak up lots of flavor from the porky broth, and the fluffy, chewy kernels released some starch, which nicely thickened the stew. Minced cilantro, stirred in at the end, added bright, fresh flavor. Pork butt roast is often labeled Boston butt in the supermarket. Serve with diced tomato, diced avocado, and thinly sliced radishes.

1 tablespoon vegetable oil

2 onions, chopped fine

2 jalapeño chiles, stemmed, seeded, and minced

⅓ cup all-purpose flour

4 garlic cloves, minced

1 tablespoon minced canned chipotle chile in adobo sauce

2 teaspoons minced fresh oregano or ½ teaspoon dried

1 cup dry white wine

2 cups chicken broth, plus extra as needed

2 (15-ounce) cans white or yellow hominy, rinsed

8 ounces carrots, peeled and sliced 1 inch thick

2 bay leaves

3 pounds boneless pork butt roast, pulled apart at seams, trimmed, and cut into 1-inch pieces

Salt and pepper

¼ cup minced fresh cilantro

Lime wedges

1 Using highest sauté or browning function, heat oil in multicooker until shimmering. Add onions and jalapeños and cook until vegetables are softened and lightly browned, 5 to 7 minutes. Stir in flour, garlic, chipotle, and oregano and cook until fragrant, about 1 minute. Slowly whisk in wine, scraping up any browned bits and smoothing out any lumps. Stir in broth, hominy, carrots, and bay leaves. Season pork with salt and pepper and stir into multicooker.

2A to pressure cook Lock lid in place and close pressure release valve. Select high pressure cook function and cook for 25 minutes. Turn off multicooker and quick-release pressure. Carefully remove lid, allowing steam to escape away from you.

2B to slow cook Lock lid in place and open pressure release valve. Select low slow cook function and cook until pork is tender, 4 to 5 hours. (If using Instant Pot, select high slow cook function and increase cooking range to 6 to 7 hours.) Turn off multicooker and carefully remove lid, allowing steam to escape away from you.

3 Discard bay leaves. Using large spoon, skim excess fat from surface of stew. Adjust consistency with extra hot broth as needed. Stir in cilantro and season with salt and pepper to taste. Serve with lime wedges.

ITALIAN VEGETABLE STEW

serves 6 to 8

pressure cook total time 1 hour	slow cook total time 6 hours 40 minutes

why this recipe works Southern Italy's vegetable stew, known as *ciambotta*, is a ratatouille-like stew that, when mopped up with a piece of crusty bread, makes a substantial, stick-to-your-ribs meal. The stew should be chock-full of vegetables—chunks of potatoes, bell peppers, onions, zucchini, eggplant, and tomatoes—that are cooked with plenty of fruity olive oil until the vegetables soften enough to thicken the tomato-rich broth. But making sure the vegetables remained bright and flavorful in the multicooker required adding our ingredients in the right order. We started by browning the chopped tomatoes, bell pepper, and onion to develop deep flavor, and then added a little tomato paste, garlic, and oregano for aromatic backbone. While eggplant often needs pretreatment such as salting to ensure a dense and creamy, not waterlogged, consistency, we found we could skip this time-consuming step and simply stir unpeeled cubes in with the potatoes. Cutting the eggplant into 1-inch pieces ensured it didn't break down too much during cooking. We simmered the delicate zucchini in the stew at the end of cooking to ensure that it remained green and crisp-tender.

¼ cup extra-virgin olive oil, plus extra for drizzling

1 (28-ounce) can whole peeled tomatoes, drained with juice reserved, chopped

1 onion, chopped fine

1 red bell pepper, stemmed, seeded, and cut into 1-inch pieces

Salt and pepper

4 garlic cloves, minced

1 tablespoon tomato paste

1 tablespoon minced fresh oregano or 1 teaspoon dried

3 cups chicken or vegetable broth, plus extra as needed

1 pound eggplant, cut into 1-inch pieces

1 pound Yukon Gold potatoes, peeled and cut into ½-inch pieces

2 zucchini, quartered lengthwise and sliced 1 inch thick

2 tablespoons chopped fresh basil

Grated Parmesan cheese

1 Using highest sauté or browning function, heat oil in multicooker until shimmering. Add tomatoes, onion, bell pepper, and ½ teaspoon salt and cook until vegetables are dry and beginning to brown, 10 to 12 minutes. Stir in garlic, tomato paste, and oregano and cook until fragrant, about 30 seconds. Stir in broth and reserved tomato juice, scraping up any browned bits, then stir in eggplant and potatoes.

2A to pressure cook Lock lid in place and close pressure release valve. Select high pressure cook function and cook for 9 minutes. Turn off multicooker and quick-release pressure. Carefully remove lid, allowing steam to escape away from you.

2B to slow cook Lock lid in place and open pressure release valve. Select low slow cook function and cook until potatoes are tender, 5 to 6 hours. (If using Instant Pot, select high slow cook function and increase cooking range to 8 to 9 hours.) Carefully remove lid, allowing steam to escape away from you.

3 Stir zucchini into stew and cook using highest sauté or browning function until tender, 8 to 10 minutes. Turn off multicooker. Adjust consistency with extra hot broth as needed. Stir in basil and season with salt and pepper to taste. Drizzle individual portions with extra oil and serve, passing Parmesan separately.

MUSHROOM AND FARRO STEW

serves 4 to 6

pressure cook total time 50 minutes	slow cook total time 3 hours 30 minutes

why this recipe works For a unique and filling stew, we turned to hearty farro and earthy mushrooms. We opted for meaty portobellos, tender creminis, and a small amount of dried porcini to give the dish a complex, balanced mushroom flavor. Tomatoes and a splash of dry sherry offered a hint of acidity that offset the richness of the mushrooms. While our stovetop version of this recipe must be stirred often, we wanted to let the multicooker do the heavy lifting and make this recipe more hands-off. But just tossing everything into the pot was a nonstarter: The mushrooms prevented the grains from cooking evenly. The answer turned out to be layering the fresh mushrooms on top of the farro so that the grains could evenly absorb the steam from the bottom of the pot. The mushrooms also gave off some of their flavorful juices, which permeated the grains nicely. We prefer the flavor and texture of whole farro. Do not use quick-cooking, presteamed, or pearled farro (read the ingredient list on the package to determine this) in this recipe. Once fully cooked, the farro will be tender but have a slight chew, similar to al dente pasta.

2 tablespoons extra-virgin olive oil, plus extra for drizzling

1 onion, chopped fine

Salt and pepper

½ ounce dried porcini mushrooms, rinsed and minced

1 teaspoon minced fresh thyme or ¼ teaspoon dried

¼ cup dry sherry

4 cups chicken or vegetable broth, plus extra as needed

1½ cups whole farro

1 (14.5-ounce) can diced tomatoes, drained and chopped

1 Parmesan cheese rind (optional), plus grated Parmesan for serving

1 pound portobello mushroom caps, gills removed, caps halved and sliced ½ inch thick

1 pound cremini mushrooms, trimmed and halved if small or quartered if large

2 tablespoons minced fresh parsley

1 Using highest sauté or browning function, heat oil in multicooker until shimmering. Add onion and ½ teaspoon salt and cook until onion is softened, 3 to 5 minutes. Stir in porcini mushrooms and thyme and cook until fragrant, about 1 minute. Stir in sherry, scraping up any browned bits, then stir in broth, farro, tomatoes, and Parmesan rind, if using. Spread portobello mushrooms and cremini mushrooms on top of farro mixture.

2A to pressure cook Lock lid in place and close pressure release valve. Select high pressure cook function and cook for 12 minutes. Turn off multicooker and quick-release pressure. Carefully remove lid, allowing steam to escape away from you.

2B to slow cook Lock lid in place and open pressure release valve. Select low slow cook function and cook until farro is tender with slight chew, 2 to 3 hours. (If using Instant Pot, select high slow cook function.) Turn off multicooker and carefully remove lid, allowing steam to escape away from you.

3 Discard Parmesan rind, if using. Adjust consistency with extra hot broth as needed. Stir in parsley and season with salt and pepper to taste. Drizzle individual portions with extra oil and serve, passing Parmesan separately.

INDIAN VEGETABLE CURRY

serves 4 to 6

pressure cook total time 45 minutes	slow cook total time 5 hours 30 minutes

why this recipe works We wanted a recipe for the ultimate vegetable curry, with a wide variety of perfectly cooked vegetables and a deeply flavorful Indian-inspired curry sauce. Curries are especially well suited to the multicooker: The closed environment means that none of the spices' volatile flavors can escape, resulting in a bold-tasting dish with plenty of complexity. To cut down on the lengthy list of spices included in many curries, we turned to flavor-packed store-bought curry powder and garam masala. We found that sautéing the spices and aromatic ingredients bloomed their flavors so they didn't taste raw in the finished dish. Choosing our curry ingredients carefully was important to making sure everything would cook through at the same time without breaking down too much. Cubed sweet potatoes and hearty cauliflower florets worked perfectly. Convenient canned chickpeas held their shape through cooking and soaked up some flavor from the sauce. We found it was necessary to hold a few ingredients out of the multicooker until after pressure or slow cooking: Green beans inevitably overcooked if added at the beginning; coconut milk maintained a brighter, fresher flavor when stirred in at the end.

3 tablespoons vegetable oil

2 onions, chopped fine

Salt and pepper

4 teaspoons curry powder

1½ teaspoons garam masala

3 garlic cloves, minced

1 serrano chile, stemmed, seeded, and minced

1 tablespoon grated fresh ginger

1 tablespoon tomato paste

2 cups chicken or vegetable broth, plus extra as needed

½ head cauliflower (1 pound), cored and cut into 1-inch florets

12 ounces sweet potatoes, peeled and cut into ¾-inch pieces

1 (15-ounce) can chickpeas, rinsed

1 (14.5-ounce) can diced tomatoes

8 ounces green beans, trimmed and cut into 1-inch lengths

½ cup canned coconut milk

⅓ cup minced fresh cilantro

1 Using highest sauté or browning function, heat oil in multicooker until shimmering. Add onions and ½ teaspoon salt and cook until onions are softened, 3 to 5 minutes. Stir in curry powder, garam masala, garlic, serrano, ginger, and tomato paste and cook until fragrant, about 1 minute. Stir in broth, scraping up any browned bits, then stir in cauliflower, potatoes, chickpeas, and tomatoes and their juice.

2A to pressure cook Lock lid in place and close pressure release valve. Select high pressure cook function and cook for 2 minutes. Turn off multicooker and quick-release pressure. Carefully remove lid, allowing steam to escape away from you.

2B to slow cook Lock lid in place and open pressure release valve. Select low slow cook function and cook until vegetables are tender, 4 to 5 hours. (If using Instant Pot, select high slow cook function and increase cooking range to 6 to 7 hours.) Carefully remove lid, allowing steam to escape away from you.

3 Gently stir green beans into curry and cook using highest sauté or browning function until crisp-tender, 6 to 8 minutes. Turn off multicooker. Stir in coconut milk and adjust consistency with extra hot broth as needed. Stir in cilantro and season with salt and pepper to taste. Serve.

CELERY ROOT, FENNEL, AND APPLE CHOWDER

serves 6

| pressure cook total time 45 minutes | slow cook total time 2 hours 30 minutes |

why this recipe works Celery root (sometimes called celeriac) is a staple in supermarkets, but most cooks walk right by it. That's a shame because this knobby tuber boasts refreshing herbal flavors with notes of anise, mint, mild radish, and celery. Its creamy (rather than starchy) texture makes it the perfect choice for a hearty vegetable chowder. To further enhance its anise flavor, we sautéed a chopped fennel bulb along with big pieces of onion. Grated apple offered subtle notes of sweetness, and chunks of tender red potatoes bulked up the chowder. For a bright citrus note, we added a strip of orange zest to the broth. To get the perfect amount of body, we pureed 2 cups of the chowder with a modest amount of cream and then stirred the puree back into the pot. Finally, we stirred in minced fresh fennel fronds for a bit of freshness.

2 tablespoons unsalted butter

1 onion, cut into ½-inch pieces

1 fennel bulb, 2 tablespoons fronds minced, stalks discarded, bulb halved, cored, and cut into ½-inch pieces

Salt and pepper

2 tablespoons all-purpose flour

6 garlic cloves, minced

2 teaspoons minced fresh thyme or ¾ teaspoon dried

½ cup dry white wine

4 cups chicken or vegetable broth

1½ cups water

14 ounces celery root, peeled and cut into ½-inch pieces

12 ounces red potatoes, unpeeled, cut into ½-inch pieces

1 Golden Delicious apple, peeled and shredded

1 bay leaf

1 (3-inch) strip orange zest

¼ cup heavy cream

1 Using highest sauté or browning function, melt butter in multicooker. Add onion, fennel pieces, and 1½ teaspoons salt and cook until vegetables are softened, 3 to 5 minutes. Stir in flour, garlic, and thyme and cook until fragrant, about 1 minute. Slowly whisk in wine, scraping up any browned bits and smoothing out any lumps, and cook until nearly evaporated, about 1 minute. Stir in broth, water, celery root, potatoes, apple, bay leaf, and orange zest.

2A to pressure cook Lock lid in place and close pressure release valve. Select high pressure cook function and cook for 3 minutes. Turn off multicooker and quick-release pressure. Carefully remove lid, allowing steam to escape away from you.

2B to slow cook Lock lid in place and open pressure release valve. Select low slow cook function and cook until vegetables are tender, 1 to 2 hours. (If using Instant Pot, select high slow cook function.) Turn off multicooker and carefully remove lid, allowing steam to escape away from you.

3 Discard bay leaf and orange zest. Transfer cream and 2 cups chowder to blender and process until smooth, about 1 minute. Stir processed chowder mixture into remaining chowder and season with salt and pepper to taste. Sprinkle individual portions with fennel fronds before serving.

EASY CHILI

serves 4 to 6

| pressure cook total time 50 minutes | slow cook total time 4 hours 30 minutes |

why this recipe works Great chili should have bold, long-simmered flavor, even if it's made with convenient ground beef. The multicooker was the perfect way to achieve this with a minimum of hands-on time. A combination of chili powder, cumin, and garlic was all we needed to give the chili great spice flavor. We used crushed tomatoes plus chicken broth for a base with the proper consistency. Browning the beef is standard in many chili recipes, but we found that the browned meat overcooked easily in either the intense heat of the pressure cooker or the prolonged heat of the slow cooker. To avoid this, we mixed it with a panade (a mixture of bread and milk) to help it stay moist, and sautéed the meat just until it lost its pink color. Serve with your favorite chili garnishes.

1 slice hearty white sandwich bread, torn into 1-inch pieces

2 tablespoons whole milk

Salt and pepper

1 pound 85 percent lean ground beef

2 tablespoons vegetable oil

1 onion, chopped fine

2 tablespoons chili powder

2 teaspoons ground cumin

4 garlic cloves, minced

1 cup chicken broth, plus extra as needed

2 (15-ounce) cans kidney beans, rinsed

1 (28-ounce) can crushed tomatoes

1 Mash bread, milk, ½ teaspoon salt, and ½ teaspoon pepper into paste in large bowl using fork. Add ground beef and knead with hands until well combined.

2 Using highest sauté or browning function, heat oil in multicooker until shimmering. Add onion and ¼ teaspoon salt and cook until onion is softened, about 5 minutes. Stir in chili powder, cumin, and garlic and cook until fragrant, about 30 seconds. Add beef mixture and cook, breaking up meat with wooden spoon, until no longer pink, about 4 minutes. Stir in broth, scraping up any browned bits, then stir in beans and tomatoes.

3A to pressure cook Lock lid in place and close pressure release valve. Select high pressure cook function and cook for 10 minutes. Turn off multicooker and quick-release pressure. Carefully remove lid, allowing steam to escape away from you.

3B to slow cook Lock lid in place and open pressure release valve. Select low slow cook function and cook until flavors meld, 3 to 4 hours. Turn off multicooker and carefully remove lid, allowing steam to escape away from you.

4 Adjust chili consistency with extra hot broth as needed. Season with salt and pepper to taste. Serve.

EASY TURKEY CHILI
Be sure to use ground turkey, not ground turkey breast (also labeled 99 percent fat-free), in this recipe.

Substitute 1 pound ground turkey for ground beef. Break turkey mixture into pieces no smaller than 1 inch when browning in step 2.

EASY FIVE-ALARM CHILI
Add 2 minced jalapeño chiles to multicooker with onions. Add ¼ cup minced canned chipotle chile in adobo and 1 teaspoon cayenne pepper to multicooker with chili powder.

CHILI CON CARNE

serves 6

| pressure cook total time 1 hour 10 minutes | slow cook total time 8 hours 30 minutes |

why this recipe works Texans are famous for their style of chili featuring hefty chunks of beef in a chile-infused sauce with creamy red beans. Beef chuck-eye roast boasted the big beefy flavor we were after and turned meltingly tender in the multicooker. To save time, we switched from dried to canned beans (with no sacrifice in texture), and found we needed to brown only half the meat to give the chili deep flavor, eliminating the need to brown in batches. To give our base the perfect consistency, we tested a variety of thickeners and landed on a nontraditional one: corn tortillas. Grinding them in the food processor ensured they melted into the chili during cooking, thickening it up perfectly without distracting from the beefy flavor. Traditional recipes call for dried chiles, but we found the multicooker did a great job of intensifying the flavors of simple, easy-to-find chili powder and canned chipotles in adobo. Serve with your favorite chili garnishes. If using an Instant Pot, do not choose the slow cook function; the beef will not cook through properly.

4 (6-inch) corn tortillas, chopped coarse

1 tablespoon vegetable oil

1 onion, chopped

1 jalapeño chile, stemmed, seeded, and minced

2 tablespoons chili powder

2 tablespoons ground cumin

5 garlic cloves, minced

1 tablespoon minced canned chipotle chile in adobo sauce

1½ cups chicken broth, plus extra as needed

1 (28-ounce) can crushed tomatoes

2 (15-ounce) cans red kidney beans, rinsed

3 pounds boneless beef chuck-eye roast, pulled apart at seams, trimmed, and cut into 1-inch pieces

Salt and pepper

Lime wedges

1 Process tortilla pieces in food processor to fine crumbs, about 30 seconds; set aside. Using highest sauté or browning function, heat oil in multicooker until shimmering. Add onion and jalapeño and cook until vegetables are softened and lightly browned, 5 to 7 minutes. Stir in chili powder, cumin, garlic, and chipotle and cook until fragrant, about 1 minute. Stir in broth, scraping up any browned bits, then stir in tomatoes and beans. Season beef with salt and pepper and stir into multicooker. Sprinkle tortilla pieces over top.

2A to pressure cook Lock lid in place and close pressure release valve. Select high pressure cook function and cook for 27 minutes. Turn off multicooker and quick-release pressure. Carefully remove lid, allowing steam to escape away from you.

2B to slow cook (Do not use Instant Pot to slow cook this recipe.) Lock lid in place and open pressure release valve. Select low slow cook function and cook until beef is tender, 7 to 8 hours. Turn off multicooker and carefully remove lid, allowing steam to escape away from you.

3 Stir chili to combine, and adjust consistency with extra hot broth as needed. Season with salt and pepper to taste. Serve, passing lime wedges separately.

BLACK BEAN CHILI

serves 4 to 6

pressure cook total time	slow cook total time
1 hour 15 minutes (plus brining time)	10 hours 30 minutes (plus brining time)

why this recipe works Black bean chili should be primarily about the beans—they should be creamy, tender, and well seasoned. We wanted a hearty bean chili that was as rich, savory, and deeply satisfying as any meat chili out there, yet simple to make in our multicooker. Tasters preferred the creamy, tender texture of dried beans over canned, and soaking the dried beans in salted water helped them hold their shape and cook evenly. Creating big flavor in vegetarian chili can be tricky since you can't use smoky ham hocks or bacon, but using the sauté function to brown a hefty amount of aromatics and bloom spices worked well to give the chili depth. We also added white mushrooms and bell peppers for body. A cup of broth and a can of crushed tomatoes provided enough liquid for our beans to cook evenly while still resulting in a thick, hearty final stew. Served with a spritz of lime and a sprinkle of minced cilantro, this rich chili was so satisfying that no one missed the meat. Serve with your favorite chili garnishes. If using an Instant Pot, do not choose the slow cook function; the beans will not cook through properly.

Salt and pepper

1 pound (2½ cups) dried black beans, picked over and rinsed

3 tablespoons vegetable oil

1 onion, chopped fine

9 garlic cloves, minced

2 tablespoons ground cumin

1½ tablespoons chili powder

1 teaspoon minced canned chipotle chile in adobo sauce

1 (28-ounce) can crushed tomatoes

1 cup chicken or vegetable broth, plus extra as needed

1 pound white mushrooms, trimmed and halved if small or quartered if large

2 red bell peppers, stemmed, seeded, and cut into ½-inch pieces

2 bay leaves

½ cup minced fresh cilantro

Lime wedges

1 Dissolve 3 tablespoons salt in 4 quarts cold water in large container. Add beans and soak at room temperature for at least 8 hours or up to 24 hours. Drain and rinse well.

2 Using highest sauté or browning function, heat oil in multicooker until shimmering. Add onion and cook until softened, 3 to 5 minutes. Stir in garlic, cumin, chili powder, and chipotle and cook until fragrant, about 1 minute. Stir in tomatoes and broth, scraping up any browned bits, then stir in beans, mushrooms, bell peppers, and bay leaves.

3A to pressure cook Lock lid in place and close pressure release valve. Select high pressure cook function and cook for 40 minutes. Turn off multicooker and quick-release pressure. Carefully remove lid, allowing steam to escape away from you.

3B to slow cook (Do not use Instant Pot to slow cook this recipe.) Lock lid in place and open pressure release valve. Select low slow cook function and cook until beans are tender, 9 to 10 hours. Turn off multicooker and carefully remove lid, allowing steam to escape away from you.

4 Discard bay leaves. Adjust consistency with extra hot broth as needed. Stir in cilantro and season with salt and pepper to taste. Serve with lime wedges.

ALL-PURPOSE CHICKEN BROTH

makes 3 quarts

pressure cook total time 2 hours 20 minutes   slow cook total time 8 hours 50 minutes

why this recipe works The multicooker is one of the home cook's best friends when it comes to homemade broth: While our stovetop broth must simmer for several hours, our broth could be done in the pressure cooker in just an hour, or could simmer the day away unattended in the slow cooker. To maximize the chicken flavor in our broth, we tested many combinations of chicken parts, finding a whole cut-up chicken too fussy and chicken backs, legs, and necks too liver-y. Chicken wings were the surprise winner—the multicooker eked out every last bit of flavor and gelatin from the chicken bones, resulting in a broth that was remarkably clear and that had a great silky texture. Browning the chicken wings was an easy way to deepen their flavor; we also browned some onion and garlic for depth. A few bay leaves were the only other seasoning we needed to complement the chicken flavor.

3 pounds chicken wings

1 tablespoon vegetable oil

1 onion, chopped

3 garlic cloves, lightly crushed and peeled

12 cups water

½ teaspoon salt

3 bay leaves

1 Pat chicken wings dry with paper towels. Using highest sauté or browning function, heat oil in multicooker for 5 minutes (or until just smoking). Brown half of chicken wings on all sides, about 10 minutes; transfer to bowl. Repeat with remaining chicken wings; transfer to bowl.

2 Add onion to fat left in multicooker and cook until softened and well browned, 8 to 10 minutes. Stir in garlic and cook until fragrant, about 30 seconds. Stir in 1 cup water, scraping up any browned bits. Stir in remaining 11 cups water, salt, bay leaves, and chicken and any accumulated juices.

3A to pressure cook Lock lid in place and close pressure release valve. Select high pressure cook function and cook for 1 hour. Turn off multicooker and let pressure release naturally for 15 minutes. Quick-release any remaining pressure, then carefully remove lid, allowing steam to escape away from you.

3B to slow cook Lock lid in place and open pressure release valve. Select low slow cook function and cook until broth is deeply flavored, 7 to 8 hours. (If using Instant Pot, select high slow cook function.) Turn off multicooker and carefully remove lid, allowing steam to escape away from you.

4 Strain broth through fine-mesh strainer into large container, pressing on solids to extract as much liquid as possible; discard solids. Using large spoon, skim excess fat from surface of broth. (Broth can be refrigerated for up to 4 days or frozen for up to 2 months.)

ALL-PURPOSE BEEF BROTH

makes 2 quarts

pressure cook total time 2 hours 50 minutes   **slow cook total time** 9 hours 50 minutes

why this recipe works Making broth from beef bones may sound like a project, but with the help of the multicooker and the microwave, it's easier than you think. The bones, which can be found in most supermarkets, give the broth great rich flavor, but many recipes call for roasting the bones in the oven for several hours first. We tried using the multicooker's sauté function to brown the bones, but the oddly shaped bones never made good contact with the hot pot. Instead, we turned to the microwave, where they browned in just 10 minutes. A splash of red wine did wonders for the color of the finished broth, and it also added some welcome acidity. In addition to the classic additions of onion, celery, and carrots, we also added mushrooms, tomato paste, and soy sauce to the pot to make the broth more savory and give it a more well-rounded flavor. A long cooking time, even under pressure, was beneficial since it gave the bones more time to release their flavor into the pot. The bones can get in the way when straining the finished broth, so remove them from the pot before straining.

2 pounds beef bones	1 celery rib, chopped	12 ounces white mushrooms, trimmed and halved
1 tablespoon vegetable oil	2 tablespoons tomato paste	1½ tablespoons soy sauce
1 small onion, chopped	½ cup dry red wine	¾ teaspoon salt
1 carrot, peeled and chopped	8 cups water	2 bay leaves

1 Arrange beef bones on paper towel–lined plate and microwave (in batches, if microwave is small) until well browned, 8 to 10 minutes.

2 Using highest sauté or browning function, heat oil in multicooker until shimmering. Add onion, carrot, and celery and cook until softened and well browned, about 18 minutes. Stir in tomato paste and cook until fragrant, about 30 seconds. Stir in wine, scraping up any browned bits, then stir in water, mushrooms, soy sauce, salt, bay leaves, and beef bones.

3A to pressure cook Lock lid in place and close pressure release valve. Select high pressure cook function and cook for 1½ hours. Turn off multicooker and let pressure release naturally for 15 minutes. Quick-release any remaining pressure, then carefully remove lid, allowing steam to escape away from you.

3B to slow cook Lock lid in place and open pressure release valve. Select low slow cook function and cook until broth is deeply flavored, 8 to 9 hours. (If using Instant Pot, select high slow cook function.) Turn off multicooker and carefully remove lid, allowing steam to escape away from you.

4 Discard bones. Strain broth through fine-mesh strainer into large container, pressing on solids to extract as much liquid as possible; discard solids. Using large spoon, skim excess fat from surface of broth. (Broth can be refrigerated for up to 4 days or frozen for up to 2 months.)

ALL-PURPOSE VEGETABLE BROTH

makes 3 quarts

pressure cook total time 2 hours 10 minutes	slow cook total time 8 hours 40 minutes

why this recipe works Vegetable broth is essential to full-flavored vegetarian cooking, enhancing meat-free dishes with clean vegetal flavor. The moist heat of the multicooker easily enhances vegetables' subtleties, making for a full-flavored broth. A base of onions, scallions, carrots, and celery along with a generous dose of garlic provided a strong backbone that was neither too vegetal nor too sweet. The addition of half a head of cauliflower, cut into florets and added with the water, gave our broth pleasant earthiness and nuttiness. Finally, a single tomato added acidic balance, and thyme sprigs, bay leaves, and peppercorns rounded out the aromatic notes. Although we wanted to be able to dump all the vegetables into the cooker raw, we found that we needed the flavor developed from browning the aromatics with the sauté function. To avoid a cloudy broth, do not press on the solids when straining.

1 tablespoon vegetable oil

3 onions, chopped

4 scallions, chopped

2 carrots, peeled and chopped

2 celery ribs, chopped

15 garlic cloves, peeled and smashed

12 cups water

½ head cauliflower (1 pound), cored and cut into 1-inch pieces

1 tomato, cored and chopped

8 sprigs fresh thyme

1 teaspoon peppercorns

½ teaspoon salt

3 bay leaves

1 Using highest sauté or browning function, heat oil in multicooker until shimmering. Add onions, scallions, carrots, celery, and garlic and cook until vegetables are softened and lightly browned, about 15 minutes. Stir in 1 cup water, scraping up any browned bits, then stir in remaining 11 cups water, cauliflower, tomato, thyme sprigs, peppercorns, salt, and bay leaves.

2A to pressure cook Lock lid in place and close pressure release valve. Select high pressure cook function and cook for 1 hour. Turn off multicooker and let pressure release naturally for 15 minutes. Quick-release any remaining pressure, then carefully remove lid, allowing steam to escape away from you.

2B to slow cook Lock lid in place and open pressure release valve. Select low slow cook function and cook until broth is deeply flavored, 7 to 8 hours. (If using Instant Pot, select high slow cook function.) Turn off multicooker and carefully remove lid, allowing steam to escape away from you.

3 Strain broth through fine-mesh strainer into large container, without pressing on solids; discard solids. (Broth can be refrigerated for up to 4 days or frozen for up to 2 months.)

EASY SUPPERS

BRAISED CHICKEN BREASTS WITH TOMATOES AND CAPERS

serves 4

pressure cook total time 1 hour	slow cook total time 2 hours 40 minutes

why this recipe works Bone-in, skin-on chicken breasts are a great candidate for multicooking: The appliance sidesteps many of the usual problems that plague white meat chicken—namely bland, dry meat—by providing a moist cooking environment that requires very little monitoring, and the bones and skin help to insulate the chicken and give it better flavor, even after high-heat pressure cooking or lengthier slow cooking. We wanted to turn our simple chicken breasts into an appealing weeknight dinner, so we decided to pair them with a vibrant, caper-spiked tomato sauce. Browning the chicken in batches rendered the excess fat and created flavorful fond. From there, we threw together our simple pantry-ready sauce. The multicooker concentrated our easy tomato sauce into something with the complexity of a much more labor-intensive sauce. While the chicken rested, we simmered the sauce briefly to thicken it to just the right consistency. If using the slow cook function, begin checking the chicken's temperature after 1 hour and continue to monitor until it is done. Serve over orzo or rice.

4 (12-ounce) bone-in split chicken breasts, trimmed

Salt and pepper

1 tablespoon extra-virgin olive oil

1 shallot, minced

1 tablespoon tomato paste

⅛ teaspoon red pepper flakes

½ cup dry white wine

1 (28-ounce) can diced tomatoes, drained

2 tablespoons capers, rinsed

¼ cup chopped fresh basil

1 Pat chicken dry with paper towels and season with salt and pepper. Using highest sauté or browning function, heat oil in multicooker for 5 minutes (or until just smoking). Place half of chicken, skin side down, in multicooker and cook until browned, 5 to 7 minutes; transfer to plate. Repeat with remaining chicken; transfer to plate.

2 Add shallot to fat left in multicooker and cook until softened, about 1 minute. Stir in tomato paste, ½ teaspoon salt, and pepper flakes and cook until fragrant, about 1 minute. Stir in wine, scraping up any browned bits, then stir in tomatoes. Nestle chicken, skin side up, into multicooker, adding any accumulated juices.

3A to pressure cook Lock lid in place and close pressure release valve. Select high pressure cook function and cook for 17 minutes. (If using Instant Pot, decrease cooking time to 9 minutes.) Turn off multicooker and quick-release pressure. Carefully remove lid, allowing steam to escape away from you.

3B to slow cook Lock lid in place and open pressure release valve. Select low slow cook function and cook until chicken registers 160 degrees, 1 to 2 hours. (If using Instant Pot, select high slow cook function.) Carefully remove lid, allowing steam to escape away from you.

4 Transfer chicken to serving dish and discard skin, if desired. Tent with aluminum foil and let rest while finishing sauce.

5 Stir capers into sauce. Using highest sauté or browning function, cook sauce, stirring occasionally, until thickened slightly and reduced to about 2 cups, 8 to 10 minutes. Season with salt and pepper to taste. Spoon sauce over chicken and sprinkle with basil. Serve.

SPANISH-STYLE CHICKEN AND COUSCOUS

serves 4

| pressure cook total time 1 hour | slow cook total time 2 hours 40 minutes |

why this recipe works Bursting with the aromatic flavors of saffron, chorizo, and garlic, this chicken and couscous dish is a winning weeknight dinner. When developing this recipe, we started with classic chicken and rice, but found that the rice was not cooking at the same rate as the chicken in the multicooker—we ended up with either stubbornly crunchy rice or egregiously overcooked chicken. Since tasters loved the Spanish flavor profile of the dish, we went in search of a different grain that would work in tandem with the chicken. A few tests revealed that couscous was the crowd favorite, and it couldn't have been simpler: Couscous doesn't require cooking at all, just soaking, which meant we could add it to the pot after pressure or slow cooking and allow it to simply absorb the ultraflavorful cooking liquid. If using the slow cook function, begin checking the chicken's temperature after 1 hour and continue to monitor until it is done.

4 (12-ounce) bone-in split chicken breasts, trimmed

Salt and pepper

1 tablespoon extra-virgin olive oil

1 red bell pepper, stemmed, seeded, and chopped fine

4 ounces Spanish-style chorizo sausage, cut into ¼-inch pieces

4 garlic cloves, minced

⅛ teaspoon saffron threads, crumbled

½ cup chicken broth

1½ cups couscous

1 cup frozen peas, thawed

2 teaspoons lemon juice

3 tablespoons minced fresh parsley

1 Pat chicken dry with paper towels and season with salt and pepper. Using highest sauté or browning function, heat oil in multicooker for 5 minutes (or until just smoking.) Place half of chicken, skin side down, in multicooker and cook until browned, 5 to 7 minutes; transfer to plate. Repeat with remaining chicken; transfer to plate.

2 Add bell pepper, chorizo, and ¼ teaspoon salt to fat left in multicooker and cook until bell pepper is softened, 3 to 5 minutes. Stir in garlic and saffron and cook until fragrant, about 30 seconds. Stir in broth, scraping up any browned bits. Nestle chicken, skin side up, into multicooker, adding any accumulated juices.

3A to pressure cook Lock lid in place and close pressure release valve. Select high pressure cook function and cook for 17 minutes. (If using Instant Pot, decrease cooking time

to 9 minutes.) Turn off multicooker and quick-release pressure. Carefully remove lid, allowing steam to escape away from you.

3B to slow cook Lock lid in place and open pressure release valve. Select low slow cook function and cook until chicken registers 160 degrees, 1 to 2 hours. (If using Instant Pot, select high slow cook function.) Turn off multicooker and carefully remove lid, allowing steam to escape away from you.

4 Transfer chicken to serving dish and discard skin, if desired. Tent with aluminum foil and let rest while preparing couscous.

5 Stir couscous, peas, and lemon juice into multicooker, cover, and let sit until couscous is tender, about 5 minutes. Add parsley and fluff couscous gently with fork to combine. Season with salt and pepper to taste. Serve with chicken.

BRAISED CHICKEN THIGHS WITH WHITE BEANS, PANCETTA, AND ROSEMARY

serves 4

pressure cook total time 50 minutes | slow cook total time 3 hours 30 minutes

why this recipe works For a Tuscan-inspired chicken dinner, we combined rich chicken thighs with bold, salty pancetta, woodsy rosemary, and creamy, mild cannellini beans. We started by browning the chicken thighs to render the fat and give the dish extra richness and savory depth, then used the fat to crisp the pancetta and brown the garlic. Canned beans worked perfectly, softening just enough in the multicooker and absorbing lots of flavor. A couple of sprigs of rosemary, added to the pot with the beans, infused the dish with subtle floral notes. This recipe was an ideal fit for the multicooker; whether pressure cooking or slow cooking, we ended up with tender, juicy meat and creamy, savory beans infused with aromatic flavor. Don't be shy with the olive oil drizzle at the end; add at least a tablespoon to each serving to boost the creaminess of the bean mixture considerably.

8 (5- to 7-ounce) bone-in chicken thighs, trimmed

Salt and pepper

1 tablespoon extra-virgin olive oil, plus extra for drizzling

2 ounces pancetta, chopped fine

5 garlic cloves, peeled and smashed

2 (15-ounce) cans cannellini beans, rinsed

½ cup water

2 sprigs fresh rosemary

1 tablespoon chopped fresh parsley

1 Pat chicken dry with paper towels and season with salt and pepper. Using highest sauté or browning function, heat oil in multicooker for 5 minutes (or until just smoking.) Place half of chicken, skin side down, in multicooker and cook until browned, 5 to 7 minutes; transfer to plate. Repeat with remaining chicken; transfer to plate.

2 Add pancetta, garlic, and ¼ teaspoon pepper to fat left in multicooker and cook until garlic is golden and pancetta is crisp and browned, about 3 minutes. Stir in beans, water, and rosemary sprigs. Nestle chicken, skin side up, into multicooker, adding any accumulated juices.

3A to pressure cook Lock lid in place and close pressure release valve. Select high pressure cook function and cook for 9 minutes. Turn off multicooker and quick-release pressure. Carefully remove lid, allowing steam to escape away from you.

3B to slow cook Lock lid in place and open pressure release valve. Select low slow cook function and cook until chicken is tender, 2 to 3 hours. (If using Instant Pot, select high slow cook function and increase cooking time to 4 to 5 hours.) Carefully remove lid, allowing steam to escape away from you.

4 Transfer chicken to serving dish and discard skin, if desired. Tent with aluminum foil and let rest while finishing beans.

5 Cook beans using highest sauté or browning function until liquid is thickened slightly, about 3 minutes. Discard rosemary sprigs. Stir in parsley and season with pepper to taste. Drizzle individual portions of beans with extra oil before serving with chicken.

CHICKEN BOUILLABAISSE

serves 4 to 6

pressure cook total time 1 hour	slow cook total time 3 hours 45 minutes

why this recipe works Although French bouillabaisse is classically made with fish, swapping in chicken made this dish perfect for the multicooker and more weeknight-friendly. The ingredients that give bouillabaisse its robust flavor, like garlic, fennel, and saffron, could withstand high pressure or hours in the slow cooker, making for an intensely flavorful broth. Browning the chicken and the aromatics helped boost savory flavor. A small amount of licorice-flavored liqueur intensified the traditional anise backbone, while canned tomatoes lent welcome acidity and brightness.

8 (5- to 7-ounce) bone-in chicken thighs, trimmed

Salt and pepper

3 tablespoons extra-virgin olive oil

1 small fennel bulb, stalks discarded, bulb halved, cored, and sliced thin

4 garlic cloves, minced

1 tablespoon tomato paste

1 tablespoon all-purpose flour

¼ teaspoon saffron threads, crumbled

¼ teaspoon cayenne pepper

¼ cup dry white wine

¼ cup pastis or Pernod

3 cups chicken broth

1 (14.5-ounce) can diced tomatoes, drained

12 ounces Yukon Gold potatoes, unpeeled, cut into ¾-inch pieces

1 (3-inch) strip orange zest

1 (12-inch) baguette, sliced ¾ inch thick on bias

1 tablespoon chopped fresh tarragon or parsley

1 Pat chicken dry with paper towels and season with salt and pepper. Using highest sauté or browning function, heat 1 tablespoon oil for 5 minutes (or until just smoking). Place half of chicken, skin side down, in multicooker and cook until browned, 5 to 7 minutes; transfer to plate. Repeat with remaining chicken; transfer to plate.

2 Add fennel to fat left in multicooker and cook until beginning to soften, about 4 minutes. Stir in garlic, tomato paste, flour, saffron, and cayenne and cook until fragrant, about 1 minute. Slowly whisk in wine and pastis, scraping up any browned bits and smoothing out any lumps. Stir in broth, tomatoes, potatoes, and orange zest. Nestle chicken, skin side up, into multicooker, adding any accumulated juices.

3A to pressure cook Lock lid in place and close pressure release valve. Select high pressure cook function and cook for 3 minutes. Turn off multicooker and quick-release pressure. Carefully remove lid, allowing steam to escape away from you.

3B to slow cook Lock lid in place and open pressure release valve. Select low slow cook function and cook until chicken is tender, 2 to 3 hours. (If using Instant Pot, select high slow cook function and increase cooking range to 4 to 5 hours.) Turn off multicooker and carefully remove lid, allowing steam to escape away from you.

4 Meanwhile, adjust oven rack to middle position and heat oven to 375 degrees. Arrange baguette slices in single layer on rimmed baking sheet. Drizzle with remaining 2 tablespoons oil and season with salt and pepper. Bake until light golden brown, 10 to 15 minutes.

5 Transfer chicken to plate and discard skin, if desired. Discard orange zest. Let cooking liquid settle, then skim excess fat from surface using large spoon. Stir in tarragon and season with salt and pepper to taste. Divide stew between individual shallow bowls and top with chicken. Serve with croutons.

TERIYAKI CHICKEN THIGHS WITH CARROTS AND SNOW PEAS

serves 4

pressure cook total time 50 minutes	slow cook total time 2 hours 30 minutes

why this recipe works For a fuss-free method that delivered a truly great chicken teriyaki—juicy meat slathered with a perfectly balanced sweet-salty glaze—we started with bone-in, skin-on chicken thighs. We seared the chicken to get some browning and get rid of excess fat. Salty soy sauce, enhanced with sugar, ginger, and garlic, not only contributed to the classic teriyaki profile, but also seasoned the chicken as it pressure or slow cooked. We used the chicken's resting time to thicken the sauce using the sauté function; a mixture of cornstarch and mirin gave the sauce a satiny texture and a bit of acidity and sweetness. Since we were already simmering the sauce, we seized the opportunity to create a complete meal by quickly cooking carrots and snow peas in the sauce as well. Mirin, a sweet Japanese rice wine, can be found in the international section of most major supermarkets and in most Asian markets. If you cannot find it, use 2 tablespoons white wine and an extra teaspoon of sugar. Serve with steamed rice.

8 (5- to 7-ounce) bone-in chicken thighs, trimmed

Pepper

1 tablespoon vegetable oil

½ cup soy sauce

½ cup sugar

½ teaspoon grated fresh ginger

1 garlic clove, minced

3 tablespoons mirin

2 tablespoons cornstarch

3 carrots, peeled and sliced thin on bias

8 ounces snow peas, strings removed

2 scallions, sliced thin on bias

1 Pat chicken dry with paper towels and season with pepper. Using highest sauté or browning function, heat oil in multicooker for 5 minutes (or until just smoking). Place half of chicken, skin side down, in multicooker and cook until browned, 5 to 7 minutes; transfer to plate. Repeat with remaining chicken; transfer to plate. Turn off multicooker and discard any fat left in multicooker.

2 Whisk soy sauce, sugar, ginger, and garlic together in now-empty multicooker, scraping up any browned bits. Nestle chicken, skin side up, into multicooker, adding any accumulated juices.

3A to pressure cook Lock lid in place and close pressure release valve. Select high pressure cook function and cook for 9 minutes. Turn off multicooker and quick-release pressure. Carefully remove lid, allowing steam to escape away from you.

3B to slow cook Lock lid in place and open pressure release valve. Select low slow cook function and cook until chicken is tender, 1 to 2 hours. (If using Instant Pot, select high slow cook function.) Carefully remove lid, allowing steam to escape away from you.

4 Transfer chicken to serving dish and discard skin, if desired. Tent with aluminum foil and let rest while cooking vegetables.

5 Whisk mirin and cornstarch in bowl until no lumps remain, then whisk mixture into sauce. Stir in carrots and cook using highest sauté or browning function until crisp-tender, about 5 minutes. Turn off multicooker. Stir in snow peas and let sit until heated through and crisp-tender, about 30 seconds. Transfer vegetable-sauce mixture to serving dish with chicken. Sprinkle with scallions and serve.

BEEF STROGANOFF

serves 4 to 6

| pressure cook total time 1 hour | slow cook total time 7 hours 30 minutes |

why this recipe works The multicooker is an ideal vessel for this classic comfort food: You can use a cheaper cut (chuck-eye roast rather than tenderloin) that has a much more intense, beefy flavor, transforming stroganoff from bland to blue ribbon. Tough chuck-eye, when cut into manageable pieces, turned meltingly tender whether cooked at high heat under pressure or gently on the slow setting. By boosting the flavor of our base with potent savory ingredients like dried porcini mushrooms, tomato paste, and soy sauce, we found that the time-consuming step of browning the meat was unnecessary: We simply browned our aromatics and mushrooms to build fond, then stirred in the seasoned beef. Since dairy curdles under pressure, we kept the sour cream out until the end and tempered it before adding it to the pot by combining it with a small amount of the warm sauce. Serve over egg noodles.

2 tablespoons vegetable oil

1½ pounds white mushrooms, trimmed and halved if small or quartered if large

3 onions, chopped fine

Salt and pepper

⅓ cup all-purpose flour

6 garlic cloves, minced

1 tablespoon tomato paste

½ ounce dried porcini mushrooms, rinsed and minced

1 tablespoon minced fresh thyme or 1 teaspoon dried

½ cup dry white wine

⅓ cup soy sauce

2 bay leaves

2 pounds boneless beef chuck-eye roast, pulled apart at seams, trimmed, and cut into 1-inch pieces

½ cup sour cream

2 teaspoons Dijon mustard

2 tablespoons minced fresh dill

1 Using highest sauté or browning function, heat oil in multicooker until shimmering. Add white mushrooms, onions, and ¼ teaspoon salt, cover, and cook until mushrooms are softened and have released their liquid, about 5 minutes. Stir in flour, garlic, tomato paste, porcini mushrooms, and thyme until incorporated and cook until fragrant, about 1 minute. Stir in wine, soy sauce, and bay leaves, scraping up any browned bits. Season beef with salt and pepper and stir into multicooker.

2A to pressure cook Lock lid in place and close pressure release valve. Select high pressure cook function and cook for 25 minutes. Turn off multicooker and quick-release pressure. Carefully remove lid, allowing steam to escape away from you.

2B to slow cook Lock lid in place and open pressure release valve. Select low slow cook function and cook until beef is tender, 6 to 7 hours. (If using Instant Pot, select high slow cook function and increase cooking range to 8 to 9 hours.) Turn off multicooker and carefully remove lid, allowing steam to escape away from you.

3 Discard bay leaves. Remove insert from multicooker and let sit for 5 minutes. Using large spoon, skim excess fat from surface of sauce. Whisk ½ cup sauce, sour cream, mustard, and dill together in bowl, then stir mixture back into multicooker. Season with salt and pepper to taste. Serve.

MUSTARD-BEER BRAISED STEAKS

serves 6

| pressure cook total time 1 hour | slow cook total time 6 hours 30 minutes |

why this recipe works Steaks are probably not the first thing you think of when you think of the multicooker, but tough blade steaks turned meltingly tender when cooked under pressure or low and slow, and they produced a sauce full of beefy flavor. To enhance the sauce for our fall-apart tender steaks, we browned our aromatics, adding potent dry mustard powder for punch and deglazing the pot with dark beer for a well-rounded, slightly malty flavor. To bring the sauce together after cooking, we gave it a spin in the blender, transforming the mixture into a velvety sauce with some rustic character. We reinforced the mustard flavor of the sauce by stirring in some whole-grain mustard at the end (when added to the pot before pressure or slow cooking, its flavor mellowed too much).

2 tablespoons extra-virgin olive oil

1 onion, chopped

1 carrot, peeled and chopped

1 celery rib, chopped

Salt and pepper

1 tablespoon dry mustard

1½ teaspoons tomato paste

1 garlic clove, minced

½ cup dark beer, such as porter or stout

3 sprigs fresh thyme

6 (6- to 8-ounce) beef blade steaks, 1 inch thick, trimmed

2 tablespoons whole-grain mustard

1 Using highest sauté or browning function, heat oil in multicooker until shimmering. Add onion, carrot, celery, and ¼ teaspoon salt and cook until vegetables are softened, 3 to 5 minutes. Stir in dry mustard, tomato paste, and garlic and cook until fragrant, about 1 minute. Stir in beer and thyme sprigs, scraping up any browned bits. Season steaks with salt and pepper and nestle into multicooker, overlapping steaks as needed.

2A to pressure cook Lock lid in place and close pressure release valve. Select high pressure cook function and cook for 35 minutes. Turn off multicooker and quick-release pressure. Carefully remove lid, allowing steam to escape away from you.

2B to slow cook Lock lid in place and open pressure release valve. Select low slow cook function and cook until steaks are tender and knife slips easily in and out of beef, 5 to 6 hours. (If using Instant Pot, select high slow cook function and increase cooking time to 6½ to 7½ hours.) Turn off multicooker and carefully remove lid, allowing steam to escape away from you.

3 Transfer steaks to serving dish, tent with aluminum foil, and let rest while finishing sauce. Discard thyme sprigs. Transfer cooking liquid and vegetables to blender. Using large spoon, skim excess fat from surface of sauce. Process sauce until smooth, about 1 minute. Add whole-grain mustard and pulse to combine, about 2 pulses. Season with salt and pepper to taste. Pour sauce over steaks and serve.

GLAZED MEATLOAF

serves 4

pressure cook total time 1 hour	slow cook total time 2 hours 40 minutes

why this recipe works Old-fashioned meatloaf is a comforting dinner, but long baking times can dry it out. The multicooker is a great way to avoid this: The moist heat and closed environment helped to alleviate dryness and ensured that the meatloaf cooked through evenly from edge to center. Meatloaf mix (a combination of ground beef, pork, and veal) made for the best, most balanced flavor. An egg gave the loaf some structure, and a panade (a paste of milk and bread) further helped the meat hold on to moisture in two ways: First, the paste physically interrupted the meat proteins from linking together into a tough matrix; and second, the paste absorbed and retained the moisture that was squeezed out from the proteins as they shrank during cooking. As for seasonings, we stuck with tradition: some sautéed onion, garlic, and thyme, along with parsley, Dijon mustard, and Worcestershire sauce. A bit of water in the bottom of the pot created a steamy environment, ensuring that the edges of the loaf didn't dry out. To make it easy to transfer the meatloaf in and out of the multicooker's deep insert, we created a foil sling. While the loaf rested, we created a simple, glaze-like sauce to pour over our finished meatloaf. If you cannot find meatloaf mix, substitute 8 ounces 85 percent lean ground beef and 8 ounces ground pork. If using the slow cook function, check the meatloaf's temperature after 1 hour of cooking and continue to monitor until it registers 155 degrees.

1 tablespoon vegetable oil	¼ cup whole milk	¼ teaspoon pepper
½ onion, chopped fine	1 large egg	1 pound meatloaf mix
2 garlic cloves, minced	2 tablespoons chopped fresh parsley	½ cup ketchup
2 teaspoons minced fresh thyme or ½ teaspoon dried	1 teaspoon Worcestershire sauce	2 tablespoons apple cider vinegar
2 slices hearty white sandwich bread, torn into ½-inch pieces	1 teaspoon Dijon mustard	2 tablespoons packed brown sugar
	1 teaspoon salt	¼ teaspoon hot sauce

1 Using highest sauté or browning function, heat oil in multicooker until shimmering. Add onion and cook until softened, 3 to 5 minutes. Stir in garlic and thyme and cook until fragrant, about 30 seconds. Turn off multicooker.

2 Transfer onion mixture to large bowl. Add bread and milk and mash into paste with fork. Stir in egg, parsley, Worcestershire, mustard, salt, and pepper. Add meatloaf mix and knead with hands until thoroughly combined.

3 Fold sheet of aluminum foil into 12 by 7-inch sling and spray with vegetable oil spray. Using wet hands, shape meat mixture into firm 7 by 4-inch loaf across center of prepared sling. Using sling, transfer meatloaf to now-empty multicooker. Pour ½ cup water around meatloaf.

4A to pressure cook Lock lid in place and close pressure release valve. Select high pressure cook function and cook for 15 minutes. Turn off multicooker and quick-release pressure. Carefully remove lid, allowing steam to escape away from you.

4B to slow cook Lock lid in place and open pressure release valve. Select low slow cook function and cook until meatloaf registers 155 degrees, 1 to 2 hours. (If using Instant Pot, select high slow cook function.) Turn off multicooker and carefully remove lid, allowing steam to escape away from you.

5 Using sling, transfer meatloaf to serving dish, allowing cooking liquid to drain back into multicooker. Remove any white albumin from meatloaf, tent with foil, and let rest while preparing glaze.

6 Discard cooking liquid and wipe multicooker clean with paper towels. Combine ketchup, vinegar, sugar, and hot sauce in now-empty multicooker and cook using highest sauté or browning function until glaze has thickened slightly, about 3 minutes. Spread glaze over meatloaf and serve.

MACARONI AND CHEESE

serves 8

| pressure cook total time 30 minutes | slow cook total time 45 minutes |

why this recipe works For mac and cheese, you're usually stuck with two options: the stuff from the box, which is easy but tastes artificial, or the lusciously cheesy casserole style that requires multiple steps of building the sauce, boiling the pasta, then marrying the two and baking it all together. With the multicooker, we could have the best of both: a simple, streamlined cooking process as well as a flavorful, ultracheesy sauce. We didn't even need to wait for a pot of water to come to a boil; we could just combine the pasta with the water (along with a bit of dry mustard and cayenne for flavor) and turn the multicooker on. The right amount of water was key to the success of this recipe. While stovetop pasta recipes call for cooking pasta in a large amount of water that then gets drained away, we needed instead to rely on the absorption method, in which the pasta absorbs most of the liquid it's cooked in. Since the multicooker is a closed environment, we didn't need to worry about evaporation, so the same amount of water could be used for the pressure setting and the slow cook setting—the pasta would always absorb the same amount of liquid, just at different rates. Because dairy curdles when cooked under pressure, we waited to add the cheese until the end. Evaporated milk thickened the sauce, and a combination of cheddar and Monterey Jack, stirred in a little at a time, melted beautifully for a creamy, cheesy mac and cheese.

1 pound elbow macaroni or small shells

3 cups water

Salt and pepper

2 teaspoons dry mustard

⅛ teaspoon cayenne pepper

2 (12-ounce) cans evaporated milk

4 ounces sharp cheddar cheese, shredded (1 cup)

4 ounces Monterey Jack cheese, shredded (1 cup)

1 Combine macaroni, water, 1½ teaspoons salt, mustard, and cayenne in multicooker.

2A to pressure cook Lock lid in place and close pressure release valve. Select high pressure cook function and cook for 5 minutes. Turn off multicooker and quick-release pressure. Carefully remove lid, allowing steam to escape away from you.

2B to slow cook Lock lid in place and open pressure release valve. Select low slow cook function and cook until macaroni is just tender, 20 to 35 minutes. Carefully remove lid, allowing steam to escape away from you.

3 Stir evaporated milk into macaroni mixture and cook using highest sauté or browning function until sauce has thickened and macaroni is fully tender, 2 to 10 minutes. Turn off multicooker. Stir in cheddar and Monterey Jack cheeses, 1 handful at a time, until cheese has melted and sauce is smooth. Season with salt and pepper to taste. Serve.

MACARONI AND CHEESE WITH BROCCOLI

Add 10 ounces broccoli florets, cut into 1-inch pieces, to multicooker with macaroni in step 1.

MACARONI AND CHEESE WITH HAM AND PEAS

Stir 8 ounces ham steak, cut into ½-inch pieces, and 1 cup frozen peas into macaroni mixture with evaporated milk.

ZITI WITH SAUSAGE RAGU

serves 4 to 6

pressure cook total time 45 minutes	slow cook total time 1 hour

why this recipe works After developing our recipe for Macaroni and Cheese (page 74) and realizing how successful pasta could be in a multicooker, we decided to take the concept one step further and develop a hearty one-pot pasta with sausage ragu. A tubular pasta like ziti proved to be the best match for the intense heat of the pressure cooker—strand pastas turned into unappealing clumps of noodles when cooked under pressure. We browned some Italian sausage, adding onion, fennel, tomato paste, garlic, and oregano for aromatic backbone. Deglazing the pot with red wine helped incorporate all the flavorful browned bits on the bottom of the pot, and letting most of the wine cook off ensured that our sauce didn't taste boozy. We then stirred in crushed tomatoes (which tasters preferred for the even-textured sauce they created), water, and our pasta. After just 5 minutes under pressure, the pasta was perfectly al dente, but even on the slow setting the dish cooked fairly quickly, making this a weeknight-friendly meal no matter which setting we used. We adjusted the sauce's consistency with a little additional water after cooking to make sure it was just the right thickness to coat our pasta. A sprinkling of basil at the end made for a fresh finish to our saucy, meaty ziti dinner.

1 tablespoon extra-virgin olive oil

1 pound hot or sweet Italian sausage, casings removed

½ fennel bulb, stalks discarded, bulb cored and chopped fine

½ onion, chopped fine

Salt and pepper

2 tablespoons tomato paste

4 garlic cloves, minced

1½ teaspoons dried oregano

¾ cup dry red wine

3½ cups water, plus extra as needed

1 (28-ounce) can crushed tomatoes

1 pound ziti

2 tablespoons shredded fresh basil

Grated Parmesan cheese

1 Using highest sauté or browning function, heat oil in multicooker until shimmering. Add sausage and cook, breaking up meat with wooden spoon, until browned, 6 to 8 minutes.

2 Stir in fennel, onion, and ½ teaspoon salt and cook until vegetables are softened, 3 to 5 minutes. Stir in tomato paste, garlic, and oregano and cook until fragrant, about 30 seconds. Stir in wine, scraping up any browned bits, and cook until nearly evaporated, about 1 minute. Stir in water, tomatoes, and pasta.

3A to pressure cook Lock lid in place and close pressure release valve. Select high pressure cook function and cook for 5 minutes. Turn off multicooker and quick-release pressure. Carefully remove lid, allowing steam to escape away from you.

3B to slow cook Lock lid in place and open pressure release valve. Select low slow cook function and cook until pasta is tender, 20 to 35 minutes. Turn off multicooker and carefully remove lid, allowing steam to escape away from you.

4 Adjust sauce consistency with extra hot water as needed. Stir in basil and season with salt and pepper to taste. Serve with Parmesan.

CHEESY ZITI WITH SAUSAGE RAGU
Before serving, dollop ½ cup whole-milk ricotta cheese over pasta and sprinkle with ½ cup shredded mozzarella. Cover multicooker and let pasta sit until mozzarella is melted, about 5 minutes.

MEATBALLS AND MARINARA

serves 4 to 6

pressure cook total time 1 hour | slow cook total time 4 hours 30 minutes

why this recipe works It's hard to find anyone who doesn't love a bowl of spaghetti topped with meatballs and marinara, but stovetop versions are often messy (between the spattering oil from frying the meatballs and the sputtering tomato sauce), and the sauce requires a long simmering time to develop rich, deep flavor. We turned to the multicooker for the neatest and most efficient method for making classic meatballs in marinara. Meatloaf mix provided a combination of ground beef, pork, and veal all in one, making our grocery list short without sacrificing flavor. The meatballs were a bit dry, so we added an egg and a panade—a paste of bread and milk—for the moisture the meatballs needed, creating tender meatballs that would also hold their shape. We seared the meatballs until they were crisp and brown; the deep pot of the multicooker kept spattering to a minimum, and the fond made a flavorful foundation for our marinara. We cooked some aromatics, added crushed tomatoes and tomato puree, and returned the meatballs to the pot. From there, we could either briefly pressure cook the mixture, or leave it unattended to gently cook for the next few hours on the slow cook setting. Either way, we never had to worry about splattering grease or sauce. The final product was a pot full of flavorful and tender yet firm meatballs in a robust, savory tomato sauce. If you cannot find meatloaf mix, substitute 8 ounces 85 percent lean ground beef and 8 ounces ground pork.

2 slices hearty white sandwich bread, torn into ½-inch pieces

¼ cup whole milk

1 ounce Parmesan cheese, grated (½ cup)

3 tablespoons minced fresh parsley

1 large egg, lightly beaten

6 garlic cloves, minced

Salt and pepper

1 pound meatloaf mix

1 tablespoon extra-virgin olive oil

2 tablespoons minced fresh oregano or 2 teaspoons dried

1 tablespoon tomato paste

1 (28-ounce) can crushed tomatoes

1 (28-ounce) can tomato puree

1 pound spaghetti

¼ cup chopped fresh basil

1 Using fork, mash bread and milk into paste in large bowl. Stir in Parmesan, parsley, egg, half of garlic, ¾ teaspoon salt, and ½ teaspoon pepper. Add meatloaf mix and knead with hands until thoroughly combined. Pinch off and roll mixture into 12 meatballs (about ¼ cup each).

2 Using highest sauté or browning function, heat oil in multicooker for 5 minutes (or until just smoking). Brown meatballs on all sides, 6 to 8 minutes; transfer to plate.

3 Add oregano, tomato paste, ¼ teaspoon salt, and remaining garlic to fat left in multicooker and cook until fragrant, about 1 minute. Stir in tomatoes and tomato puree, scraping up any browned bits. Gently nestle meatballs into sauce, adding any accumulated juices.

4A to pressure cook Lock lid in place and close pressure release valve. Select high pressure cook function and cook for 15 minutes. Turn off multicooker and quick-release pressure. Carefully remove lid, allowing steam to escape away from you.

4B to slow cook Lock lid in place and open pressure release valve. Select low slow cook function and cook until meatballs are tender, 3 to 4 hours. (If using Instant Pot, select high slow cook function and increase cooking range to 4 to 5 hours.) Turn off multicooker and carefully remove lid, allowing steam to escape away from you.

5 Meanwhile, bring 4 quarts water to boil in large pot. Add pasta and 1 tablespoon salt and cook, stirring often, until al dente. Reserve ½ cup cooking water, then drain pasta and return it to pot. Add several spoonfuls of sauce (without meatballs) and basil and toss to combine. Add reserved cooking water as needed to adjust consistency. Serve pasta with remaining sauce and meatballs.

RAGU ALLA BOLOGNESE

serves 4 to 6

why this recipe works Rich, deeply flavorful Bolognese sauce is usually out of reach on a weeknight, but we wanted to use the multicooker to change that. For the ultimate ultrasavory, velvety Bolognese in the multicooker, we started with the star of the recipe: the meat. We used a combination of ground beef, ground pork, and ground veal for the best flavor, as well as some chopped pancetta and mortadella to give the sauce even more depth. A basic trio of vegetables—onion, carrot, and celery—gave the sauce a nice backbone when we browned them with the meat. The food processor made short work of chopping the vegetables, the pancetta, and the mortadella. Since tomatoes should play second fiddle to the meat in this sauce, we used a can of tomato paste for deep yet subtle tomato flavor. Red wine offered acidity and rounded flavor. Since store-bought broth lacks the body of homemade, we doctored up our store-bought broth with powdered gelatin. Although our recipe required a bit of work up front, once we turned the multicooker on, our work was nearly done: After cooking, we simply stirred in some chicken livers (ground in the food processor) for even more depth and complexity. This recipe makes enough sauce to coat 2 pounds of pasta. Leftover sauce can be refrigerated for up to three days or frozen for up to one month. If you can't find ground veal, use an additional 12 ounces of ground beef.

½ cup chicken broth

½ cup beef broth

6 teaspoons unflavored gelatin

1 onion, chopped coarse

1 large carrot, peeled and chopped coarse

1 celery rib, chopped coarse

4 ounces pancetta, chopped

4 ounces mortadella, chopped

6 ounces chicken livers, trimmed

3 tablespoons extra-virgin olive oil

12 ounces 85 percent lean ground beef

12 ounces ground pork

12 ounces ground veal

3 tablespoons minced fresh sage

1 (6-ounce) can tomato paste

1 cup dry red wine

Salt and pepper

1 pound pappardelle or tagliatelle

Grated Parmesan cheese

1 Combine chicken broth and beef broth in bowl. Sprinkle gelatin over broth mixture and let sit until gelatin softens, about 5 minutes.

2 Pulse onion, carrot, and celery in food processor until finely chopped, about 10 pulses, scraping down sides of bowl as needed; transfer to separate bowl. Pulse pancetta and mortadella in now-empty processor until finely chopped, about 25 pulses; transfer to third bowl. Process chicken livers in now-empty processor until pureed, about 5 seconds; refrigerate until ready to use.

3 Using highest sauté or browning function, heat oil in multicooker until shimmering. Add beef, pork, veal, and pancetta mixture and cook, breaking up meat with wooden spoon, until all liquid has evaporated and meat begins to sizzle, 10 to 15 minutes. Add chopped vegetables, sage, and tomato paste and cook, stirring frequently, until vegetables begin to soften and tomato paste is fragrant, about 3 minutes. Stir in wine, scraping up any browned bits, and cook until mostly evaporated, about 30 seconds. Stir in broth mixture.

4A to pressure cook Lock lid in place and close pressure release valve. Select high pressure cook function and cook for 20 minutes. Turn off multicooker and quick-release pressure. Carefully remove lid, allowing steam to escape away from you.

4B to slow cook Lock lid in place and open pressure release valve. Select low slow cook function and cook until meat is tender, 3 to 4 hours. (If using Instant Pot, select high slow cook function and increase cooking range to 7 to 8 hours.) Turn off multicooker and carefully remove lid, allowing steam to escape away from you.

5 Stir chicken livers into sauce and let sit for 3 minutes. Season with salt and pepper to taste; cover to keep warm.

6 Meanwhile, bring 4 quarts water to boil in large pot. Add pasta and 1 tablespoon salt and cook, stirring often, until al dente. Reserve ¾ cup cooking water, then drain pasta and return it to pot. Add half of sauce and reserved cooking water, and toss to combine. Serve with Parmesan.

SOUTHERN-STYLE SMOTHERED PORK CHOPS

serves 4

| pressure cook total time 1 hour | slow cook total time 3 hours 45 minutes |

why this recipe works "Smothered" pork chops, which are cooked in a rich gravy until the meat is fall-off-the-bone tender, are a classic Southern dish. We knew the multicooker would be the perfect way to achieve a thick gravy and moist chops with great flavor. We started by choosing the best type of pork chops, landing on thick-cut bone-in blade chops; their higher fat content made them a perfect candidate for multicooking, since their collagen melts easily into gelatin during pressure or slow cooking. To give the chops and the gravy bold flavor without having to add a pantry full of spices, we made a simple mixture of Lawry's Seasoned Salt (a Southern favorite), onion powder, garlic powder, paprika, and pepper, and we used the mixture in three places: on the chops, in the flour dredge for the chops, and in the gravy. We first browned the coated chops on one side and then built a gravy in the multicooker pot by adding flour right to the rendered pork fat. We cooked the roux until it was the color of peanut butter so that our gravy would have great depth of flavor. We nestled the chops into the gravy to cook, then allowed them to rest while we thickened the gravy and stirred in a bit of cider vinegar for brightness.

2 tablespoons Lawry's Seasoned Salt

1 tablespoon onion powder

1 teaspoon garlic powder

1 teaspoon paprika

Pepper

4 (8- to 10-ounce) bone-in blade-cut pork chops, ¾ to 1 inch thick, trimmed

¾ cup all-purpose flour

2 tablespoons vegetable oil

2 onions, quartered through root end and sliced thin crosswise

1¾ cups water

1 tablespoon cider vinegar

1 Combine seasoned salt, onion powder, garlic powder, paprika, and 1 teaspoon pepper in bowl. Cut 2 slits about 2 inches apart through fat on edges of each chop. Pat chops dry with paper towels and sprinkle each chop with 1 teaspoon spice mixture (½ teaspoon per side).

2 Combine ½ cup flour and 4 teaspoons spice mixture in shallow dish. Dredge 1 side of chops lightly in seasoned flour, shake off excess, and transfer to plate.

3 Using highest sauté or browning function, heat oil in multicooker for 5 minutes (or until just smoking). Place half of chops floured side down into multicooker and cook until well-browned on 1 side, 3 to 5 minutes; return to plate. Repeat with remaining chops; transfer to plate.

4 Stir remaining ¼ cup flour into fat left in multicooker. Cook, stirring constantly, until roux is color of peanut butter, 3 to 5 minutes. Add onions and remaining spice mixture and cook, stirring constantly, until onions begin to soften slightly, about 2 minutes. Slowly stir in water, scraping up any browned bits and smoothing out any lumps. Nestle chops into multicooker, adding any accumulated juices.

5A to pressure cook Lock lid in place and close pressure release valve. Select high pressure cook function and cook for 15 minutes. Turn off multicooker and quick-release pressure. Carefully remove lid, allowing steam to escape away from you.

5B to slow cook Lock lid in place and open pressure release valve. Select low slow cook function and cook until meat is tender, 2 to 3 hours. (If using Instant Pot, select high slow cook function and increase cooking range to 4 to 5 hours.) Carefully remove lid, allowing steam to escape away from you.

6 Transfer chops to serving dish, tent with aluminum foil, and let rest while finishing sauce. Cook sauce using highest sauté or browning function until thickened, 3 to 5 minutes. Turn off multicooker. Let sauce settle, then skim excess fat from surface using large spoon. Stir in vinegar and season with pepper to taste. Spoon sauce over chops and serve.

BRAISED SAUSAGES WITH LENTILS AND KALE

serves 4

| pressure cook total time 1 hour | slow cook total time 3 hours 30 minutes |

why this recipe works For a hearty yet simple dinner, we turned to flavorful Italian sausage, toothsome lentils, and earthy kale. Cooking the sausages and lentils together in the multicooker infused the lentils with meaty flavor. We browned the sausages first to boost the savoriness of the dish, then added some aromatics, chicken broth, and the lentils. Whether we used the intense heat of the pressure cooker or the extended stay in the slow cooker, regular brown lentils tended to soften a bit too much and fall apart, so we opted instead for smaller, firmer French green lentils. The French lentils held their shape nicely, no matter which cooking method we chose. After cooking, we set the sausages aside to rest and briefly simmered some kale with the lentils until the greens were just wilted while still maintaining their fresh bite. French green lentils (*lentilles du Puy*) work best in this recipe; do not use large brown or green lentils.

1 tablespoon extra-virgin olive oil

1½ pounds hot or sweet Italian sausage

2 shallots, peeled, halved, and sliced thin

3 garlic cloves, minced

1 teaspoon minced fresh thyme or ¼ teaspoon dried

1 cup chicken broth

1 cup water

1 cup French green lentils, picked over and rinsed

2 tablespoons whole-grain mustard

Pepper

12 ounces kale, stemmed and chopped coarse

1 Using highest sauté or browning function, heat oil in multicooker for 5 minutes (or until just smoking). Brown sausages on all sides, 6 to 8 minutes; transfer to plate.

2 Add shallots to fat left in multicooker and cook until softened, about 1 minute. Stir in garlic and thyme and cook until fragrant, about 30 seconds. Stir in broth, water, lentils, mustard, and ¼ teaspoon pepper. Nestle sausages into multicooker, adding any accumulated juices.

3A to pressure cook Lock lid in place and close pressure release valve. Select high pressure cook function and cook for 25 minutes. Turn off multicooker and quick-release pressure. Carefully remove lid, allowing steam to escape away from you.

3B to slow cook Lock lid in place and open pressure release valve. Select low slow cook function and cook until lentils are tender, 2 to 3 hours. (If using Instant Pot, select high slow cook function and increase cooking time to 6 to 7 hours.) Carefully remove lid, allowing steam to escape away from you.

4 Transfer sausages to serving dish, tent with aluminum foil, and let rest while finishing lentils. Stir kale into lentils, 1 handful at a time, and cook using highest sauté or browning function until wilted and tender, about 3 minutes. Season with pepper to taste. Serve with sausages.

POACHED SALMON WITH CUCUMBER AND TOMATO SALAD

serves 4

pressure cook total time 25 minutes	slow cook total time 45 minutes

why this recipe works Cooking salmon can be intimidating since it overcooks and dries out so easily. But the multicooker makes the process foolproof: The consistent moisture level and temperature, as well as the precise timing safeguards against overcooking, produce evenly cooked salmon each and every time. Cooking the salmon on a foil sling made it easy to transfer in and out of the multicooker, and propping the fish up on lemon slices insulated it from the direct heat. While both methods produced great salmon in under an hour, we slightly preferred the slow cook setting since it allowed us to regularly check the doneness of the fish, guaranteeing that it was cooked perfectly. To complete our healthy dinner, we made a fresh and light salad with cucumber, tomatoes, olives, and herbs. If using the slow cook function, check the salmon's temperature after 15 minutes of cooking and continue to monitor until it registers 135 degrees.

1 lemon, sliced ¼ inch thick, plus 1 teaspoon grated lemon zest and 2 tablespoons juice

¼ cup fresh parsley leaves, stems reserved

1 tablespoon chopped fresh dill, stems reserved

1 (1½-pound) skinless center-cut salmon fillet, 1 to 1½ inches thick, sliced crosswise into 4 equal pieces

Salt and pepper

3 tablespoons extra-virgin olive oil

1 shallot, minced

2 tablespoons capers, rinsed and minced

1 English cucumber, halved lengthwise and sliced thin

8 ounces cherry tomatoes, halved

¾ cup pitted kalamata olives, halved

1 Fold sheet of aluminum foil into 12 by 9-inch sling. Press sling into multicooker, allowing narrow edges to rest along sides of insert. Arrange lemon slices in single layer on prepared sling, then scatter parsley and dill stems over top. Add water until liquid level is even with lemon slices (about ½ cup). Season salmon with salt and pepper and arrange skinned side down in even layer on top of herb stems.

2A to pressure cook Lock lid in place and close pressure release valve. Select high pressure cook function and cook for 5 minutes. Turn off multicooker and quick-release pressure. Carefully remove lid, allowing steam to escape away from you.

2B to slow cook Lock lid in place and open pressure release valve. Select low slow cook function and cook until salmon is opaque throughout when checked with tip of paring knife

and registers 135 degrees (for medium), 15 to 20 minutes. (If using Instant Pot, select high slow cook function.) Turn off multicooker and carefully remove lid, allowing steam to escape away from you.

3 Meanwhile, whisk oil, shallot, capers, lemon zest and juice, and chopped dill together in large bowl. Add cucumber, tomatoes, olives, and parsley leaves and gently toss to combine. Season with salt and pepper to taste.

4 Using sling, transfer salmon to baking sheet; discard poaching liquid. Gently lift and tilt fillets with spatula to remove herb stems and lemon slices and remove any white albumin. Transfer salmon to individual plates and serve with salad.

SHRIMP WITH PARMESAN FARROTTO

serves 6

| pressure cook total time 1 hour | slow cook total time 2 hours 20 minutes |

why this recipe works Italian *farrotto* is a risotto-style dish made with farro in place of the usual Arborio rice, creating a hearty and warming dish. To make it a full meal, we decided to take advantage of the ample residual heat in the pot after pressure or slow cooking to gently cook some delicate shrimp. But first we needed to get our farrotto's texture right: Achieving a creamy, velvety consistency with farro can be a challenge, since much of the grains' starch is trapped inside the outer bran. Cracking the farro in a blender freed up enough starch to create the appropriate risotto-like consistency. Since the multicooker is a closed environment and no liquid evaporates during cooking, we could simply add a measured amount of liquid up front, eliminating much of the guesswork involved in traditional risotto. A bit of garlic, thyme, and white wine offered an aromatic backbone, and plenty of Parmesan cheese made the finished farrotto extra creamy and savory. Do not use quick-cooking, presteamed, or pearled farro (read the ingredient list on the package to determine this) in this recipe. Once fully cooked, the farro will be tender but have a slight chew, similar to al dente pasta.

1½ cups whole farro

4 tablespoons unsalted butter

½ onion, chopped fine

Salt and pepper

1 garlic clove, minced

2 teaspoons minced fresh thyme or ½ teaspoon dried

¼ cup dry white wine

2½ cups chicken broth, plus extra as needed

1 pound medium-large shrimp (31 to 40 per pound), peeled, deveined, and tails removed

2 ounces Parmesan cheese, grated (1 cup)

2 tablespoons minced fresh parsley

2 teaspoons lemon juice

1 Pulse farro in blender until about half of grains are broken into smaller pieces, about 6 pulses.

2 Using highest sauté or browning function, melt 2 tablespoons butter in multicooker. Add onion, 1 teaspoon salt, and ¾ teaspoon pepper and cook until onion is softened, about 3 minutes. Stir in farro, garlic, and thyme and cook until fragrant, about 1 minute. Stir in wine and cook until nearly evaporated, about 30 seconds. Stir in broth.

3A to pressure cook Lock lid in place and close pressure release valve. Select high pressure cook function and cook for 15 minutes. Turn off multicooker and quick-release pressure. Carefully remove lid, allowing steam to escape away from you.

3B to slow cook Lock lid in place and open pressure release valve. Select low slow cook function and cook until farro is tender, 1 to 2 hours. (If using Instant Pot, select high slow cook function.) Turn off multicooker and carefully remove lid, allowing steam to escape away from you.

4 Stir shrimp into farrotto, cover, and let sit until opaque throughout, 6 to 8 minutes. Add Parmesan and remaining 2 tablespoons butter and stir vigorously until farrotto becomes creamy. Adjust consistency with extra hot broth as needed. Stir in parsley and lemon juice and season with salt and pepper to taste. Serve.

THAI BRAISED EGGPLANT

serves 4

| pressure cook total time 35 minutes | slow cook total time 4 hours 30 minutes |

why this recipe works To create a hearty, vegetable-packed Thai-style curry, we turned to creamy Japanese eggplant as the star ingredient. To avoid waterlogged eggplant, we needed to drive off its excess moisture before braising. The multicooker let us do just that: We sautéed the eggplant right in the multicooker pot. We then built a flavorful, aromatic base with garlic, ginger, lemon grass, and simple, flavorful store-bought green curry paste. Sweet red bell peppers complemented the savory eggplant, and to ensure that the peppers turned out perfectly crisp-tender, we didn't brown them with the other ingredients, instead adding them to the mix right before placing the lid on the multicooker. Stirring in coconut milk at the end of cooking gave our curry a creamy, velvety texture. Soy sauce, fish sauce, and lime juice cut through the richness of the coconut milk, and a sprinkling of scallion greens brightened the finished dish.

3 tablespoons vegetable oil

2 pounds Japanese eggplant, sliced into 1-inch-thick rounds

8 garlic cloves, minced

6 scallions, white and green parts separated and sliced thin

2 tablespoons Thai green curry paste

2 tablespoons grated fresh ginger

1 lemon grass stalk, trimmed to bottom 6 inches and bruised with back of knife

3 red bell peppers, stemmed, seeded, and cut into 1-inch pieces

½ cup chicken or vegetable broth

1 (14-ounce) can coconut milk

¼ cup minced fresh cilantro

4 teaspoons lime juice

1 tablespoon soy sauce

2 teaspoons fish sauce (optional)

1 Using highest sauté or browning function, heat 1 tablespoon oil in multicooker until shimmering. Brown half of eggplant on all sides, about 6 minutes; transfer to bowl. Repeat with 1 tablespoon oil and remaining eggplant; transfer to bowl.

2 Add garlic, scallion whites, curry paste, ginger, lemon grass, and remaining 1 tablespoon oil to now-empty multicooker and cook until fragrant, about 30 seconds. Stir in eggplant and any accumulated juices, peppers, and broth.

3A to pressure cook Lock lid in place and close pressure release valve. Select high pressure cook function and cook for 5 minutes. Turn off multicooker and quick-release pressure. Carefully remove lid, allowing steam to escape away from you.

3B to slow cook Lock lid in place and open pressure release valve. Select low slow cook function and cook until eggplant is tender, 3 to 4 hours. (If using Instant Pot, select high slow cook function and increase cooking range to 4 to 5 hours.) Turn off multicooker and carefully remove lid, allowing steam to escape away from you.

4 Discard lemon grass. Stir in coconut milk, cilantro, lime juice, soy sauce, and fish sauce, if using. Sprinkle individual portions with scallion greens before serving.

SPAGHETTI SQUASH WITH FRESH TOMATO SAUCE

serves 4

pressure cook total time **50 minutes**	slow cook total time **5 hours 30 minutes**

why this recipe works Delicately flavored spaghetti squash makes for a fun and interesting vegetarian main, but often the squash must be roasted in the oven while a separate sauce is made on the stove. In the multicooker, however, we could make a simple fresh tomato sauce and cook a large 4-pound spaghetti squash together in one pot. First, we bloomed aromatic garlic, oregano, and pepper flakes with tomato paste to provide our sauce with a deeply flavored base. We opted for plum tomatoes for our sauce; because they contain less juice compared with larger tomatoes and less skin compared with an equal amount of small cherry tomatoes, we didn't need to worry about seeding or peeling, saving time. Finally, we added the squash, halved and seeded, to the pot, and cooked it until it was tender. We found that the liquid from the tomatoes was enough to steam our squash to perfection, but to rid the final dish of excess moisture, we drained the shredded squash in a strainer and further reduced and concentrated the sauce using the sauté function. A sprinkling of fresh basil and shaved Parmesan cheese completed the plate.

3 tablespoons extra-virgin olive oil

3 garlic cloves, minced

1 tablespoon tomato paste

1 teaspoon minced fresh oregano or ½ teaspoon dried

Pinch red pepper flakes

Salt and pepper

2 pounds plum tomatoes, cored and cut into 1-inch pieces

1 (4-pound) spaghetti squash, halved lengthwise and seeded

2 tablespoons chopped fresh basil

Shaved Parmesan

1 Using highest sauté or browning function, heat oil in multi-cooker until shimmering. Add garlic, tomato paste, oregano, pepper flakes, and ½ teaspoon salt and cook, stirring frequently, until fragrant, about 30 seconds. Stir in tomatoes. Season squash halves with salt and pepper and nestle cut side down into multicooker.

2A to pressure cook Lock lid in place and close pressure release valve. Select high pressure cook function and cook for 10 minutes. Turn off multicooker and quick-release pressure. Carefully remove lid, allowing steam to escape away from you.

2B to slow cook Lock lid in place and open pressure release valve. Select low slow cook function and cook until squash is tender, 4 to 5 hours. (If using Instant Pot, select high slow cook function and increase cooking range to 5 to 6 hours.) Carefully remove lid, allowing steam to escape away from you.

3 Transfer squash to cutting board, let cool slightly, then shred flesh into strands using 2 forks; discard skins. Transfer squash to fine-mesh strainer and let drain while finishing sauce.

4 Cook sauce using highest sauté or browning function until tomatoes are completely broken down and sauce is thickened, 15 to 20 minutes. Transfer squash to serving dish, spoon sauce over top, and sprinkle with basil and Parmesan. Serve.

ROASTS AND RIBS

CHICKEN IN A POT WITH LEMON-HERB SAUCE

serves 4

pressure cook total time 1 hour	slow cook total time 4 hours 30 minutes

why this recipe works Cooking a whole chicken in a moist covered environment isn't a new concept. In fact, the classic French method of cooking *en cocotte* relies on this principle to create unbelievably tender, moist meat and a savory sauce enhanced with the chicken's own concentrated juices. We knew this would be a perfect use for the multicooker, and started with a 4-pound chicken, which fit nicely into the narrow pot. Since we wanted to focus on achieving succulent meat and not on getting crisp skin, we didn't bother with the time-consuming step of browning the chicken; sautéing some onion and garlic in the pot gave the chicken and the *jus* layers of deep flavor. Both pressure and slow cooking produced a chicken with perfectly cooked light and dark meat. A couple of tablespoons of flour, added at the start, ensured that our jus was transformed into a velvety smooth sauce after cooking. Butter, lemon juice, and fresh herbs gave our sauce a final boost of rich, bright flavor. If using the slow cook function, begin checking the chicken's temperature after 3 hours and continue to monitor until it is done.

1 tablespoon vegetable oil

1 onion, chopped fine

2 tablespoons all-purpose flour

3 garlic cloves, minced

2 teaspoons minced fresh rosemary

½ cup dry white wine

1 cup chicken broth

1 (4-pound) whole chicken, giblets discarded

Salt and pepper

2 tablespoons unsalted butter, cut into 2 pieces and chilled

2 tablespoons lemon juice

¼ cup minced fresh chives, parsley, or tarragon

1 Using highest sauté or browning function, heat oil in multicooker until shimmering. Add onion and cook until softened, 3 to 5 minutes. Stir in flour, garlic, and rosemary and cook until fragrant, about 1 minute. Slowly whisk in wine, scraping up any browned bits and smoothing out any lumps, then stir in broth. Season chicken with salt and pepper and place breast side up into multicooker.

2A to pressure cook Lock lid in place and close pressure release valve. Select high pressure cook function and cook for 30 minutes. Turn off multicooker and quick-release pressure. Carefully remove lid, allowing steam to escape away from you.

2B to slow cook Lock lid in place and open pressure release valve. Select low slow cook function and cook until breast registers 160 degrees and thighs register 175 degrees, 3 to 4 hours. (If using Instant Pot, select high slow cook function.) Turn off multicooker and carefully remove lid, allowing steam to escape away from you.

3 Transfer chicken to carving board, tent with aluminum foil, and let rest for 5 to 10 minutes. Let cooking liquid settle, then skim excess fat from surface using large spoon. Whisk in butter, lemon juice, and chives. Carve chicken, discarding chicken skin if desired. Serve with sauce.

SPICED CHICKEN IN A POT WITH PEAR, CHERRY, AND WALNUT CHUTNEY

serves 4

| pressure cook total time 1 hour 45 minutes | slow cook total time 5 hours |

why this recipe works This recipe gives you a sophisticated, company-worthy entrée of warm-spiced chicken and a sweet-savory chutney—all made in your multicooker. Rubbing a whole chicken with spices is always a great way to infuse it with bold flavor; the spices' nuanced flavors were brought out by the multicooker's concentrated heat, whether we used the pressure or the slow setting, and the tight-fitting lid ensured that no flavor escaped during cooking. For even more depth of flavor, we browned the chicken before locking on the lid. For an elegant accompaniment, we decided on a pear, cherry, and walnut chutney. Since chutneys taste best when their flavors are allowed time to meld before serving, we decided to use the multicooker to cook our chutney before cooking the chicken. We used the sauté function to lightly brown the pears, then added shallot, ginger, and cherry preserves to give the chutney a thick, jammy texture. A healthy dose of white wine vinegar balanced the sweetness of the pears and cherry preserves. To maintain the textural contrast of the crunchy toasted walnuts, we waited to add them until after cooking the chutney. If using the slow cook function, begin checking the chicken's temperature after 3 hours and continue to monitor until it is done.

3 tablespoons vegetable oil

1½ pounds ripe but firm Bosc or Bartlett pears, peeled, halved, cored, and cut into ½-inch pieces

1 shallot, minced

1 tablespoon grated fresh ginger

Salt and pepper

½ cup cherry preserves

⅓ cup white wine vinegar

2 tablespoons water

¼ cup walnuts, toasted and chopped

2 teaspoons five-spice powder

1½ teaspoons ground cumin

1 teaspoon garlic powder

¼ teaspoon cayenne pepper

¼ teaspoon ground cardamom

1 (4-pound) whole chicken, giblets discarded

1 Using highest sauté or browning function, heat 1 tablespoon oil in multicooker until shimmering. Cook pears until softened and lightly browned, 8 to 10 minutes. Stir in shallot, ginger, and ¼ teaspoon salt and cook until fragrant, about 1 minute. Stir in cherry preserves, vinegar, and water and cook until thickened and mixture measures about 1½ cups, 6 to 8 minutes. Turn off multicooker. Transfer chutney to bowl and stir in walnuts; set aside for serving. (Chutney can be refrigerated for up to 1 week; bring to room temperature before serving.) Wipe multicooker clean with paper towels.

2 Combine 1 tablespoon oil, 2 teaspoons salt, five-spice powder, cumin, 1 teaspoon pepper, garlic powder, cayenne, and cardamom in small bowl. Pat chicken dry with paper towels and, using your fingers, gently loosen skin covering breast and thighs. Rub spice paste evenly over and under skin.

3 Using highest sauté or browning function, heat remaining 1 tablespoon oil in multicooker for 5 minutes (or until just smoking). Place chicken, breast side down, in multicooker

and cook until well browned, 6 to 8 minutes. Using tongs, gently flip chicken and cook until well browned on second side, 6 to 8 minutes. Add 1 cup water to multicooker.

4A to pressure cook Lock lid in place and close pressure release valve. Select high pressure cook function and cook for 27 minutes. Turn off multicooker and quick-release pressure. Carefully remove lid, allowing steam to escape away from you.

4B to slow cook Lock lid in place and open pressure release valve. Select low slow cook function and cook until breast registers 160 degrees and thighs register 175 degrees, 3 to 4 hours. (If using Instant Pot, select high slow cook function.) Turn off multicooker and carefully remove lid, allowing steam to escape away from you.

5 Transfer chicken to carving board, tent with aluminum foil, and let rest for 5 to 10 minutes. Carve chicken, discarding skin if desired. Serve with chutney.

CLASSIC POT ROAST WITH MUSHROOM GRAVY

serves 6 to 8

pressure cook total time 2 hours 15 minutes	slow cook total time 8 hours 45 minutes

why this recipe works Pot roast is one of the best examples of what the moist, even heat of a multicooker can do: A notoriously tough cut is made tender, flavorful, and comforting. We started with our favorite cut for pot roast, chuck-eye roast, since its generous marbling translates into great beefy flavor. To fit a roast large enough to feed 6 to 8 people, we found it was best to cut the roast in half; this created two smaller roasts that cooked much more consistently and fit more easily in the narrow multicooker pot. As an added bonus, the smaller roasts took less time to cook. Searing them in the multicooker was crucial in developing the rich and savory flavor that we craved. We enhanced the cooking liquid with aromatics like onion and thyme to give our pot roast a classic flavor profile. By adding some flour and sliced cremini mushrooms to the pot, we found we could effortlessly create a thick, luscious gravy along with the meat—all we needed to do was let the gravy reduce while the roasts rested after cooking. When pressure cooking, we found that a natural release was essential to keep the meat tender. Whether we chose high-heat pressure cooking or gentle slow cooking, our pot roast and gravy rivaled the best versions made on the stovetop.

1 (3½- to 4-pound) boneless beef chuck-eye roast, pulled into 2 pieces at natural seam and trimmed

Salt and pepper

2 tablespoons vegetable oil

1 onion, chopped

¼ cup all-purpose flour

1 tablespoon tomato paste

1 teaspoon minced fresh thyme or ¼ teaspoon dried

½ cup dry red wine

1 cup beef broth

1 pound cremini mushrooms, trimmed and sliced thin

2 bay leaves

2 tablespoons minced fresh parsley

1 Pat beef dry with paper towels and season with salt and pepper. Tie 3 pieces of kitchen twine around each piece of beef to create 2 evenly shaped roasts. Using highest sauté or browning function, heat oil in multicooker for 5 minutes (or until just smoking). Brown roasts on all sides, 8 to 10 minutes; transfer to plate.

2 Add onion to fat left in multicooker and cook until softened, 3 to 5 minutes. Stir in flour, tomato paste, and thyme and cook until fragrant, about 1 minute. Slowly whisk in

wine, scraping up any browned bits and smoothing out any lumps. Stir in broth, mushrooms, and bay leaves. Nestle roasts into multicooker, adding any accumulated juices.

3A to pressure cook Lock lid in place and close pressure release valve. Select high pressure cook function and cook for 65 minutes. Turn off multicooker and let pressure release naturally for 15 minutes. Quick-release any remaining pressure, then carefully remove lid, allowing steam to escape away from you.

3B to slow cook Lock lid in place and open pressure release valve. Select low slow cook function and cook until beef is tender and knife slips easily in and out of meat, 7 to 8 hours. (If using Instant Pot, select high slow cook function and increase cooking range to 10 to 11 hours.) Turn off multicooker and carefully remove lid, allowing steam to escape away from you.

4 Transfer roasts to carving board, tent with aluminum foil, and let rest while finishing gravy.

5 Discard bay leaves. Using highest sauté or browning function, cook gravy for 5 to 10 minutes, until slightly thickened. Turn off multicooker. Let gravy settle, then skim excess fat from surface using large spoon. Season with salt and pepper to taste. Remove twine from roasts and slice against grain into ½-inch-thick slices. Arrange beef on serving dish, spoon 1 cup gravy over top, and sprinkle with parsley. Serve, passing remaining gravy separately.

ONION-BRAISED BEEF BRISKET

serves 8 to 10

pressure cook total time 4 hours 30 minutes | slow cook total time 10 hours

why this recipe works The multicooker has the ability to produce meltingly tender brisket and a flavorful sauce, but getting there requires a few tricks. We started with a flat cut brisket, which we halved to make it easier to fit in the multicooker. Browning both halves built up a savory base for our braising liquid, and by further amping up the braising liquid's flavor with lots of aromatics, it could later double as a luxurious serving sauce. We softened a generous 2½ pounds of onions in the rendered fat from the meat, adding garlic, tomato paste, paprika, cayenne, and plenty of herbs to round out the flavor. A combination of broth and wine added savory depth and brightness. Our brisket needed a long cooking time, whether we cooked it on the pressure setting or the slow setting, to become fully tender, but our real breakthrough came when we left the brisket in the turned-off multicooker for an extra hour: This rest time allowed the meat to soak up some of the liquid it had lost during cooking, leading to a moister, more sliceable texture. After the brisket's rest, we took it out of the pot and used the sauté function to reduce the sauce to the right consistency before serving.

1 (3½- to 4-pound) beef brisket, flat cut, fat trimmed to ¼ inch, halved crosswise

Salt and pepper

1 tablespoon vegetable oil

2½ pounds onions, halved and sliced ½ inch thick

3 garlic cloves, minced

1 tablespoon tomato paste

1 tablespoon paprika

⅛ teaspoon cayenne pepper

½ cup chicken broth

½ cup dry red wine

3 bay leaves

3 sprigs fresh thyme

2 teaspoons cider vinegar

1 Pat brisket dry with paper towels and place fat side up on cutting board. Using fork, poke holes in meat through fat layer about 1 inch apart. Season with salt and pepper.

2 Using highest sauté or browning function, heat oil in multi-cooker for 5 minutes (or until just smoking). Place 1 brisket half fat side down in multicooker and cook until well browned, about 8 minutes. Flip brisket and cook until well browned on second side, 3 to 5 minutes; transfer to large plate. Repeat with second brisket half; transfer to plate.

3 Add onions and ¼ teaspoon salt to fat left in multicooker and cook until onions are softened, 10 to 12 minutes. Stir in garlic, tomato paste, paprika, and cayenne and cook until fragrant, about 1 minute. Stir in broth, wine, bay leaves, and

thyme sprigs, scraping up any browned bits. Nestle brisket halves into onion mixture (pieces will overlap), adding any accumulated juices.

4A to pressure cook Lock lid in place and close pressure release valve. Select high pressure cook function and cook for 1½ hours. Turn off multicooker and let pressure release naturally for 15 minutes. Quick-release any remaining pressure and let brisket sit, covered, for 1 hour. Carefully remove lid, allowing steam to escape away from you.

4B to slow cook Lock lid in place and open pressure release valve. Select low slow cook function and cook until beef is tender and knife slips easily in and out of meat, 6½ to 7½ hours. (If using Instant Pot, select high slow cook function and

increase cooking range to 10 to 11 hours.) Turn off multi-cooker and let brisket sit, covered, for 1 hour. Carefully remove lid.

5 Transfer brisket to carving board and tent with aluminum foil. Strain braising liquid through fine-mesh strainer into bowl. Discard bay leaves and thyme sprigs. Reserve onions in separate bowl. Let liquid settle, then skim excess fat from surface using large spoon. Return liquid to multicooker and cook using highest sauté or browning function until reduced to about 2 cups, 15 to 20 minutes.

6 Slice brisket against grain into ¼-inch-thick slices and place slices on serving dish. Stir reserved onions and vinegar into sauce, and season with salt and pepper to taste. Spoon sauce over brisket and serve.

RUSTIC ITALIAN BRAISED BEEF SHORT RIBS

serves 4

pressure cook total time 2 hours 15 minutes | slow cook total time 8 hours 45 minutes

why this recipe works In this recipe, bone-in short ribs are transformed into a luxurious, saucy dish reminiscent of a traditional Sunday gravy. The multicooker does a great job of extracting all the gelatin from the bones, so the cooking liquid becomes a supersilky sauce. We started by using the sauté function to soften onions and then bloom tomato paste, garlic, oregano, and red pepper flakes to develop big flavor. We added canned diced tomatoes and a small amount of water before nestling the short ribs into the sauce base. Whether we used the pressure or the slow setting, the long cooking time turned the ribs perfectly tender and thickened the sauce beautifully. A generous amount of fresh basil finished the dish on a bright note. Serve with polenta or pasta.

1 tablespoon extra-virgin olive oil

2 onions, chopped

Salt and pepper

10 garlic cloves, sliced thin

1 tablespoon tomato paste

1 tablespoon minced fresh oregano or 1 teaspoon dried

½ teaspoon red pepper flakes

2 (15-ounce) cans diced tomatoes

½ cup water

3 pounds bone-in English-style short ribs, 1½ to 2 inches thick, 2 inches wide, and 4 to 5 inches long, trimmed

¼ cup chopped fresh basil

1 Using highest sauté or browning function, heat oil in multicooker until shimmering. Add onions and ¼ teaspoon salt and cook until onions are softened and lightly browned, 5 to 7 minutes. Stir in garlic, tomato paste, oregano, and pepper flakes and cook until fragrant, about 1 minute. Stir in tomatoes and water, scraping up any browned bits. Season short ribs with salt and pepper and nestle into multicooker.

2A to pressure cook Lock lid in place and close pressure release valve. Select high pressure cook function and cook for 60 minutes. Turn off multicooker and let pressure release naturally for 15 minutes. Quick-release any remaining pressure, then carefully remove lid, allowing steam to escape away from you.

2B to slow cook Lock lid in place and open pressure release valve. Select low slow cook function and cook until beef is tender and knife slips easily in and out of meat, 7 to 8 hours. (If using Instant Pot, select high slow cook function and increase cooking range to 9 to 10 hours.) Carefully remove lid, allowing steam to escape away from you.

3 Transfer short ribs to serving dish, tent with aluminum foil, and let rest while finishing sauce.

4 Using highest sauté or browning function, cook sauce until slightly thickened, 10 to 15 minutes. Turn off multicooker. Let sauce settle, then skim excess fat from surface using large spoon. Stir in basil and season with salt and pepper to taste. Spoon 1 cup sauce over short ribs and serve, passing remaining sauce separately.

TAMARIND BRAISED BEEF SHORT RIBS

serves 4

| pressure cook total time 2 hours 45 minutes | slow cook total time 7 hours 45 minutes |

why this recipe works Beefy short ribs pair perfectly with intensely flavored sauces, so for this recipe we opted for sweet-tart tamarind as a foil to the ultrarich meat. Boneless ribs were well suited to serving whole with a drizzle-able sauce, so we started there. To make our sauce, we browned some onion and garlic, then added easy-to-find tamarind juice concentrate, along with white wine for acidity, soy sauce for depth, and brown sugar and warm spices for a rounded flavor. Without the extra gelatin from the bones, our flavorful sauce needed some additional body after pressure or slow cooking, so we finished it with a cornstarch slurry for a supple texture. Look for lean ribs cut from the chuck. If you need to buy bone-in English-style ribs, slice off the bones, cartilage, and excess fat. If your short ribs are a single slab, cut them into 1½-inch-wide strips. Serve with rice.

1 tablespoon vegetable oil

1 onion, chopped

2 garlic cloves, minced

Salt and pepper

½ cup dry white wine

⅓ cup tamarind juice concentrate

2 tablespoons soy sauce

2 tablespoons packed dark brown sugar

2 cinnamon sticks

1 teaspoon allspice berries

2½ pounds boneless short ribs, 1½ to 2 inches thick, 1 to 1½ inches wide, and 4 to 5 inches long, trimmed

¼ cup water

1 tablespoon cornstarch

1 tablespoon balsamic vinegar

1 tablespoon shredded fresh basil

1 Using highest sauté or browning function, heat oil in multicooker until shimmering. Add onion and cook until softened and lightly browned, 5 to 7 minutes. Stir in garlic and 1 teaspoon pepper and cook until fragrant, about 30 seconds. Stir in wine, tamarind juice, soy sauce, sugar, cinnamon sticks, and allspice berries, scraping up any browned bits. Season short ribs with pepper and nestle into multicooker.

2A to pressure cook Lock lid in place and close pressure release valve. Select high pressure cook function and cook for 95 minutes. Turn off multicooker and let pressure release naturally for 15 minutes. Quick-release any remaining pressure, then carefully remove lid, allowing steam to escape away from you.

2B to slow cook Lock lid in place and open pressure release valve. Select low slow cook function and cook until beef is tender and knife slips easily in and out of meat, 6 to 7 hours.

(If using Instant Pot, select high slow cook function and increase cooking range to 8 to 9 hours.) Turn off multicooker and carefully remove lid, allowing steam to escape away from you.

3 Transfer short ribs to serving dish, tent with aluminum foil, and let rest while finishing sauce.

4 Strain braising liquid through fine-mesh strainer into fat separator and let settle for 5 minutes. Return defatted liquid to now-empty multicooker and cook using highest sauté or browning function until reduced to about 1 cup, 10 to 15 minutes. Whisk water and cornstarch together in bowl, then whisk mixture into sauce and continue to cook until thickened, about 1 minute. Turn off multicooker. Stir in vinegar and season with salt and pepper to taste. Spoon sauce over short ribs, sprinkle with basil, and serve.

OSSO BUCO WITH SWEET AND SPICY PEPERONATA

serves 6

pressure cook total time 2 hours 15 minutes	slow cook total time 8 hours 45 minutes

why this recipe works *Ossobuco* is a famous Italian dish of tender braised veal shanks and vegetables topped with a bright, piquant *gremolata* (a mix of garlic, citrus peel, and parsley). We set out to create a modern spin on this dish using our multicooker. Veal shanks were a perfect fit for this appliance: They became remarkably moist and supple thanks to the multicooker's ability to draw out their plentiful collagen and transform it into gelatin. To serve six people, we used good-size shanks and tied them around the equator to keep the meat attached to the bones. Browning the shanks in two batches built savory fond and prevented overcrowding in the multicooker, while deglazing the pan with wine enhanced the flavor of the meat. While the finishing dollop of gremolata usually does the work of offsetting some of the veal's richness, we decided on a different Italian specialty: a sweet and spicy *peperonata*, a classic condiment of stewed bell peppers, onions, and tomatoes, which we brightened up with capers and caper brine. We tried cooking our peperonata with the veal shanks, but tasters thought the peppers became too soft and lost their brightness with the extended cooking time. Instead, we kept the veal cooking liquid very simple—just wine, thyme, garlic, and a bay leaf—then cooked our peperonata at the end, while the veal shanks rested. Just 15 minutes using the sauté function were enough to meld the peperonata's flavors while keeping everything fresh-tasting. Serve with risotto, polenta, or mashed potatoes.

6 (14- to 16-ounce) veal shanks, 1½ inches thick, trimmed and tied around equator

Salt and pepper

¼ cup extra-virgin olive oil

3 sprigs fresh thyme

8 garlic cloves, minced

¾ cup dry white wine

1 bay leaf

4 red or yellow bell peppers, stemmed, seeded, and cut into ¼-inch-wide strips

1 onion, halved and sliced thin

1 (14.5-ounce) can diced tomatoes, drained

¼ cup raisins

2 tablespoons tomato paste

¼ teaspoon red pepper flakes

2 tablespoons capers plus 4 teaspoons caper brine

½ cup chopped fresh basil

1 Pat shanks dry with paper towels and season with salt and pepper. Using highest sauté or browning function, heat 2 tablespoons oil in multicooker for 5 minutes (or until just smoking). Brown half of shanks on 1 side, 4 to 6 minutes; transfer to plate. Repeat with remaining shanks; transfer to plate.

2 Add thyme sprigs and half of garlic to fat left in multicooker and cook until fragrant, about 30 seconds. Stir in wine and bay leaf, scraping up any browned bits. Nestle shanks into multicooker (shanks will overlap slightly), adding any accumulated juices.

3A to pressure cook Lock lid in place and close pressure release valve. Select high pressure cook function and cook for 60 minutes. Turn off multicooker and let pressure release naturally for 15 minutes. Quick-release any remaining pressure, then carefully remove lid, allowing steam to escape away from you.

3B to slow cook Lock lid in place and open pressure release valve. Select low slow cook function and cook until veal is tender and knife slips easily in and out of meat, 7 to 8 hours. (If using Instant Pot, select high slow cook function and increase cooking range to 10 to 11 hours.) Turn off multicooker and carefully remove lid, allowing steam to escape away from you.

4 Transfer shanks to serving dish and discard twine. Tent with aluminum foil and let rest while cooking peperonata. Discard cooking liquid and wipe multicooker clean with paper towels.

5 Using highest sauté or browning function, heat remaining 2 tablespoons oil in multicooker until shimmering. Add bell peppers, onion, tomatoes, raisins, tomato paste, pepper flakes, ¼ teaspoon salt, and remaining garlic. Cover and cook, stirring occasionally, until vegetables are softened, 10 to 15 minutes. Turn off multicooker. Stir in capers and brine and season with salt and pepper to taste. Spoon peperonata over shanks and sprinkle with basil. Serve.

PORK LOIN WITH BLACK MOLE SAUCE

serves 6

| pressure cook total time 1 hour | slow cook total time 2 hours 45 minutes |

why this recipe works Pork loin roasts are perfect blank canvases for intensely flavored sauces, so we decided to pair our roast with a rich, complex mole sauce. Mole sauces are usually cooked separately from the meat, meaning lots of dishes to wash after dinner. But with the multicooker we could cook the pork and the sauce at the same rate in only one vessel, streamlining prep. We decided to create a mole *negro*, or black mole sauce, which contains dried chiles, spices, cocoa, tomatillos, tomatoes, and dried fruit, along with nuts and seeds for body. We toasted the chiles right in the multicooker pot, which deepened their flavor and saved us from having to dirty an additional pan. To make sure the roast cooked evenly, we cut it in half (this also helped it fit into smaller 6-quart multicookers), and we cut the tomatoes and tomatillos into relatively large pieces and placed the pork on top so that it wasn't submerged in liquid. We blended the sauce after cooking to achieve its hallmark velvety consistency. For the moistest meat, we strongly recommend brining the pork in a solution of 2 quarts cold water, ¼ cup salt, and ¼ cup sugar for 1½ to 2 hours before cooking. If only "enhanced" pork is available (the label will state that the pork was injected with a water-salt solution), do not brine the pork. If using the slow cook function, begin checking the pork's temperature after 1 hour and continue to monitor until it is done. Serve with rice.

3 pasilla chiles, stemmed, seeded, and torn into ½-inch pieces (¾ cup)

1 (2½- to 3-pound) boneless pork loin roast, trimmed, halved crosswise, and brined if desired

1 tablespoon vegetable oil

1 onion, chopped

Salt and pepper

2 garlic cloves, minced

2 teaspoons minced fresh oregano or ½ teaspoon dried

⅛ teaspoon ground cloves

⅛ teaspoon ground cinnamon

1 cup chicken broth, plus extra as needed

1 tomato, cored and quartered

8 ounces tomatillos, husks and stems removed, rinsed well, dried, and halved

3 tablespoons dry-roasted peanuts

2 tablespoons sesame seeds, toasted

2 tablespoons raisins

1 tablespoon unsweetened cocoa powder

1 Using highest sauté or browning function, toast pasillas in multicooker, stirring frequently, until fragrant, 2 to 6 minutes; transfer to bowl.

2 Tie 3 pieces of kitchen twine around each piece of pork to create 2 evenly shaped roasts. Heat oil in now-empty multicooker until shimmering. Add onion and 1 teaspoon salt and cook until onion is softened, 3 to 5 minutes. Stir in garlic, oregano, cloves, and cinnamon and cook until

fragrant, about 30 seconds. Stir in broth, scraping up any browned bits. Stir in tomato, tomatillos, peanuts, 1 tablespoon sesame seeds, raisins, cocoa, pasillas, and ½ teaspoon pepper. Place roasts fat side up on top of tomato-tomatillo mixture so they sit above liquid.

3A to pressure cook Lock lid in place and close pressure release valve. Select high pressure cook function and cook for 14 minutes. Turn off multicooker and let pressure release

naturally for 15 minutes. Quick-release any remaining pressure, then carefully remove lid, allowing steam to escape away from you.

3B to slow cook Lock lid in place and open pressure release valve. Select low slow cook function and cook until pork is tender and registers 145 degrees, 1 to 2 hours. (If using Instant Pot, select high slow cook function.) Turn off multicooker and carefully remove lid, allowing steam to escape away from you.

4 Transfer pork to carving board, tent with aluminum foil, and let rest for 5 to 10 minutes.

5 Transfer cooking liquid to blender and process until smooth, 1 to 2 minutes. Adjust consistency with extra hot broth as needed. Season with salt and pepper to taste. Remove twine from roasts, slice into ¼-inch-thick slices, and transfer to serving dish. Spoon 1 cup sauce over pork and sprinkle with remaining 1 tablespoon sesame seeds. Serve, passing remaining sauce separately.

CIDER-BRAISED PORK POT ROAST

serves 8

pressure cook total time 2 hours 50 minutes	slow cook total time 9 hours 15 minutes

why this recipe works Pork and apples are a classic combination, so we set out to create a recipe for a pork roast that would braise in a cider-based sauce and result in a tender roast infused with sweet-tart cider flavor. We started with pork butt—a great cut for braising in the multicooker since it turns silky and tender with either high-heat pressure cooking or extended slow cooking. Searing the meat (cut into two pieces to fit in the narrow pot) built a flavorful and appealing deep golden crust and created valuable fond in the pot that added flavor to our sauce. Once the roasts were cooked, we decided to make use of their resting time, cooking some sliced apples in a bit of the rendered pork fat until they were browned and tender. We then stirred in some of the strained cooking liquid, and also whisked in apple butter and a slurry of cornstarch and cider to help thicken the sauce and reinforce the bright apple flavor. Pork butt roast is often labeled Boston butt in the supermarket. If using an Instant Pot, do not choose the slow cook function; the pork will not cook through properly.

1 (4-pound) boneless pork butt roast, trimmed and halved

Salt and pepper

2 tablespoons vegetable oil

1 onion, halved and sliced thin

6 garlic cloves, peeled and smashed

6 sprigs fresh thyme

2 bay leaves

1 cinnamon stick

2 cups apple cider

2 Braeburn or Jonagold apples, cored and cut into 6 wedges each

¼ cup apple butter

1 tablespoon cornstarch

1 tablespoon cider vinegar

1 Pat pork dry with paper towels and season with salt and pepper. Tie 3 pieces of kitchen twine around each piece of pork to create 2 evenly shaped roasts. Using highest sauté or browning function, heat oil in multicooker for 5 minutes (or until just smoking). Brown 1 roast on all sides, 8 to 10 minutes; transfer to plate. Repeat with remaining roast; transfer to plate.

2 Add onion to fat left in multicooker and cook until softened and lightly browned, 5 to 7 minutes. Stir in garlic, thyme sprigs, bay leaves, and cinnamon stick and cook until fragrant, about 30 seconds. Stir in 1¾ cups cider, scraping up any browned bits. Nestle roasts fat side up into multicooker, adding any accumulated juices.

3A to pressure cook Lock lid in place and close pressure release valve. Select high pressure cook function and cook for 60 minutes. Turn off multicooker and let pressure release naturally for 15 minutes. Quick-release any remaining pressure, then carefully remove lid, allowing steam to escape away from you.

3B to slow cook (Do not use Instant Pot to slow cook this recipe.) Lock lid in place and open pressure release valve. Select low slow cook function and cook until pork is tender and knife slips easily in and out of meat, 7 to 8 hours. Turn off multicooker and carefully remove lid, allowing steam to escape away from you.

4 Transfer roasts to carving board, tent with aluminum foil, and let rest while finishing apples and sauce. Strain braising liquid through fine-mesh strainer into fat separator; discard solids and let liquid settle for at least 5 minutes. Wipe multicooker clean with paper towels.

5 Spoon 1½ tablespoons of clear, separated fat from top of fat separator into now-empty multicooker and heat using highest sauté or browning function until shimmering. Season apples with salt and pepper. Space apples evenly in multicooker, cut side down, and cook until softened and well browned on both cut sides, 6 to 8 minutes; transfer to serving dish and tent with foil.

6 Return 2 cups defatted braising liquid to now-empty multicooker and bring to boil. Whisk in apple butter until incorporated. Whisk cornstarch and remaining ¼ cup cider together in bowl, then whisk mixture into sauce and continue to cook until slightly thickened, about 1 minute. Turn off multicooker. Stir in vinegar and season with salt and pepper to taste.

7 Remove twine from roasts and slice against grain into ½-inch-thick slices. Arrange pork on serving dish with apples and spoon 1 cup sauce over top. Serve, passing remaining sauce separately.

SHREDDED PORK SOFT TACOS

serves 6 to 8

pressure cook total time 1 hour 45 minutes	slow cook total time 4 hours

why this recipe works Tender shredded pork butt makes for a flavorful and indulgent taco filling. However, our usual method requires braising the pork in a heavy Dutch oven (which must be moved to and from the oven), then transferring the pork to a bowl to shred it, and finally broiling it on a wire rack in a rimmed baking sheet to achieve the hallmark crisp edges on the pork. The results are great: moist, fall-apart pork infused with bright citrus flavor. But the pile of dishes left behind makes this essentially simple recipe into a project. Translating the recipe for the multicooker streamlined it: We could build an aromatic base, braise the pork, and crisp the cooked meat all in one vessel. We cut the pork into small pieces before putting it in the pot. The pieces became so tender during cooking that we didn't even need to shred them; they simply broke down when we stirred. Orange juice and zest, chipotle chile in adobo, and a halved onion (which we removed after cooking) gave the pork a traditional, aromatic flavor. To crisp the meat after pressure or slow cooking, we simply cooked it uncovered until the liquid evaporated so the meat could brown. Some lime juice, added at the end, enhanced the bright citrus flavor of the pork. Cilantro and thinly sliced radishes added freshness, color, and crunch to our tacos. Pork butt roast is often labeled Boston butt in the supermarket.

1 (3- to 4-pound) boneless pork butt roast, pulled apart at seams, trimmed, and cut into 2-inch pieces

6 (3-inch) strips orange zest plus ½ cup juice

2 onions (1 onion halved through root end, 1 onion chopped fine)

1 tablespoon minced canned chipotle chile in adobo sauce

1 tablespoon minced fresh oregano or 1 teaspoon dried

1 tablespoon sugar

1 teaspoon ground cumin

Salt and pepper

1 bay leaf

2 tablespoons lime juice, plus lime wedges for serving

18 (6-inch) corn tortillas, warmed

Fresh cilantro leaves

Thinly sliced radishes

1 Combine pork, orange zest and juice, halved onion, chipotle, oregano, sugar, cumin, 1 teaspoon salt, ½ teaspoon pepper, and bay leaf in multicooker.

2A to pressure cook Lock lid in place and close pressure release valve. Select high pressure cook function and cook for 25 minutes. Turn off multicooker and let pressure release naturally for 15 minutes. Quick-release any remaining pressure, then carefully remove lid, allowing steam to escape away from you.

2B to slow cook Lock lid in place and open pressure release valve. Select low slow cook function and cook until pork is tender, 2 to 3 hours. (If using Instant Pot, select high slow cook function and increase cooking range to 7 to 8 hours.) Turn off multicooker and carefully remove lid, allowing steam to escape away from you.

3 Discard orange zest, onion halves, and bay leaf. Let braising liquid settle, then skim excess fat from surface using large spoon. Cook pork, uncovered, using highest sauté or browning function until liquid is mostly reduced, 20 to 30 minutes. Continue to cook, stirring occasionally to break up pork, until liquid has completely evaporated and pork begins to crisp around edges, about 10 minutes. Stir lime juice into pork and season with salt and pepper to taste. Serve pork with warm tortillas, chopped onion, cilantro, radishes, and lime wedges.

NORTH CAROLINA—STYLE PULLED PORK

serves 8

| pressure cook total time 1 hour 45 minutes | slow cook total time 6 hours 45 minutes |

why this recipe works Great North Carolina pulled pork should consist of succulent, smoky meat napped in a tangy vinegar-based sauce. But traditional recipes can require a full day of closely monitoring a grill. To streamline this often labor-intensive dish without losing out on any of the flavor, we started with a traditional pork butt roast. The moist heat of the multicooker effortlessly tenderized this tough cut. The only thing the multicooker couldn't do was give the meat its characteristic smoky flavor, but this was an easy fix: We added liquid smoke to the braising liquid—no grill required. We infused the pork with classic barbecue flavors by rubbing it with a sweet and spicy dry rub made with brown sugar, paprika, chili powder, cumin, salt, and pepper. We also used our simple homemade sauce as our braising liquid, which had the added benefit of deepening the flavor of the sauce. Once the pork was cooked, we removed it from the pot to shred it and reduced the sauce to a thick, clingy consistency. Don't shred the meat too fine in step 3; it will break up more as the meat is combined with the sauce. Pork butt roast is often labeled Boston butt in the supermarket.

3 tablespoons packed brown sugar, plus extra as needed

2 tablespoons paprika

2 tablespoons chili powder

2 teaspoons ground cumin

Salt and pepper

1 (4-pound) boneless pork butt roast, trimmed and quartered

¾ cup plus 1 tablespoon cider vinegar, plus extra for seasoning

½ cup water

½ cup ketchup

½ teaspoon liquid smoke

8 hamburger buns

1 Combine sugar, paprika, chili powder, cumin, 1½ teaspoons salt, and ½ teaspoon pepper in bowl, then rub mixture evenly over pork. Combine ¾ cup vinegar, water, ketchup, and liquid smoke in multicooker, then nestle pork into multicooker.

2A **to pressure cook** Lock lid in place and close pressure release valve. Select high pressure cook function and cook for 45 minutes. Turn off multicooker and let pressure release naturally for 15 minutes. Quick-release any remaining pressure, then carefully remove lid, allowing steam to escape away from you.

2B **to slow cook** Lock lid in place and open pressure release valve. Select low slow cook function and cook until pork is tender and knife slips easily in and out of meat, 5 to 6 hours.

(If using Instant Pot, select high slow cook function and increase cooking range to 9 to 10 hours.) Turn off multicooker and carefully remove lid, allowing steam to escape away from you.

3 Transfer pork to large bowl, let cool slightly, then shred into bite-size pieces, discarding any excess fat.

4 Let braising liquid settle, then skim excess fat from surface using large spoon. Using highest sauté or browning function, cook liquid until reduced to about 2 cups, 15 to 20 minutes. Stir in remaining 1 tablespoon vinegar and season with salt, pepper, extra sugar, and extra vinegar to taste. Stir 1 cup sauce into shredded pork, then add extra sauce to taste. Serve shredded pork on buns, passing remaining sauce separately.

CHINESE BARBECUED SPARERIBS

serves 4 to 6

pressure cook total time 2 hours	slow cook total time 5 hours 15 minutes

why this recipe works Chinese barbecued spareribs should be seasoned to the bone, with sweet-savory lacquered exteriors. We like to use the multicooker for ribs since the moist, trapped heat produces perfectly tender meat every time. Cutting the ribs apart before cooking made them easier to fit into the multicooker and encouraged each rib to absorb maximum flavor from our braising liquid. Plenty of potent ingredients packed a flavor punch. To achieve a sticky yet crisp coating on the ribs, we reduced the sauce in the multicooker, then tossed the ribs in the sauce before roasting them in the oven. These ribs are meant to be chewier than American-style barbecued ribs. It's not necessary to remove the membrane that runs along the bone side of the ribs. This recipe was developed using an 8-quart multicooker. If using the pressure cook function on a 6-quart multicooker, decrease cook time to 5 minutes. If using an Instant Pot, do not choose the slow cook function; the ribs will not cook through properly.

1 (6-inch) piece ginger, peeled and sliced thin

8 garlic cloves, peeled

1 cup honey

¾ cup hoisin sauce

¾ cup soy sauce

½ cup water

½ cup Shaoxing rice wine or dry sherry

2 teaspoons five-spice powder

1 teaspoon ground white pepper

1 teaspoon red food coloring (optional)

2 (2½- to 3-pound) racks St. Louis–style spareribs, cut into individual ribs

2 tablespoons toasted sesame oil

1 Pulse ginger and garlic in food processor until finely chopped, 10 to 12 pulses, scraping down sides of bowl as needed; transfer to multicooker. Whisk in honey, hoisin, soy sauce, water, rice wine, five-spice powder, pepper, and food coloring, if using, until combined. Add ribs and toss to coat (ribs will not be fully submerged).

2A to pressure cook Lock lid in place and close pressure release valve. Select high pressure cook function and cook for 8 minutes. Turn off multicooker and let pressure release naturally for 15 minutes. Quick-release any remaining pressure, then carefully remove lid, allowing steam to escape away from you.

2B to slow cook (Do not use Instant Pot to slow cook this recipe.) Lock lid in place and open pressure release valve. Select low slow cook function and cook until ribs are just tender, 3 to 4 hours. Turn off multicooker and carefully remove lid, allowing steam to escape away from you.

3 Transfer ribs to large plate. Strain braising liquid through fine-mesh strainer into large bowl, pressing on solids to extract as much liquid as possible; discard solids. Let braising liquid settle, then skim excess fat from surface using large spoon. Return liquid to multicooker and add oil. Using highest sauté or browning function, cook until reduced to about 2½ cups, about 25 minutes.

4 Adjust oven rack to middle position and heat oven to 425 degrees. Set wire rack in aluminum foil–lined rimmed baking sheet and pour ½ cup water in bottom of sheet. Place half of ribs in glaze and gently toss to coat. Transfer ribs bone side up to prepared sheet, letting excess glaze drip off.

5 Roast until edges of ribs start to caramelize, 5 to 7 minutes. Flip ribs over and continue to cook until second side starts to caramelize, 5 to 7 minutes. Transfer ribs to serving dish and repeat glazing and roasting of remaining ribs. Serve, passing any remaining glaze separately.

LAMB SHANKS WITH FIGS AND NORTH AFRICAN SPICES

serves 6

pressure cook total time 2 hours 30 minutes **slow cook total time** 8 hours

why this recipe works Lamb shanks are ideal for multicooking: The moist heat breaks down the shanks' collagen-rich connective tissue to produce fall-apart-tender meat. Since lamb shanks have such robust flavor, we wanted our braising liquid to double as an equally bold serving sauce. Browning the shanks added complex flavor to the dish. We bloomed some North African spices in the lamb's rendered fat, and added sweet dried figs to balance out the dish's savory notes. While the shanks rested, we reduced the braising liquid into a satiny sauce. To avoid a greasy dish, be sure to trim the shanks of all visible fat and to defat the sauce thoroughly. Serve with couscous.

6 (10- to 12-ounce) lamb shanks, trimmed

Salt and pepper

2 tablespoons extra-virgin olive oil

1 onion, chopped fine

2 tablespoons tomato paste

2 garlic cloves, minced

1 teaspoon ground coriander

½ teaspoon ground cumin

½ teaspoon ground cinnamon

⅛ teaspoon cayenne pepper

½ cup dry red wine

1 (14.5-ounce) can diced tomatoes

¾ cup dried figs, stemmed and halved

½ cup chicken broth

2 tablespoons honey

2 tablespoons minced fresh mint

1 Pat shanks dry with paper towels and season with salt and pepper. Using highest sauté or browning function, heat oil in multicooker for 5 minutes (or until just smoking). Brown half of shanks on all sides, 8 to 10 minutes; transfer to plate. Repeat with remaining shanks; transfer to plate.

2 Add onion and ¼ teaspoon salt to fat left in multicooker and cook until onion is softened and lightly browned, 5 to 7 minutes. Stir in tomato paste, garlic, coriander, cumin, cinnamon, and cayenne and cook until fragrant, about 1 minute. Stir in wine, scraping up any browned bits, then stir in tomatoes and their juice, figs, and broth. Nestle shanks into multicooker, adding any accumulated juices.

3A to pressure cook Lock lid in place and close pressure release valve. Select high pressure cook function and cook for 60 minutes. Turn off multicooker and let pressure release naturally for 15 minutes. Quick-release any remaining pressure, then carefully remove lid, allowing steam to escape away from you.

3B to slow cook Lock lid in place and open pressure release valve. Select low slow cook function and cook until lamb is tender and knife slips easily in and out of meat, 6 to 7 hours. (If using Instant Pot, select high slow cook function and increase cooking range to 10 to 11 hours.) Carefully remove lid, allowing steam to escape away from you.

4 Transfer shanks to serving dish, tent with aluminum foil, and let rest while finishing sauce.

5 Using highest sauté or browning function, cook sauce until slightly thickened, 8 to 10 minutes. Turn off multicooker. Let sauce settle, then skim excess fat from surface using large spoon. Stir in honey and season with salt and pepper to taste. Spoon 1 cup sauce over shanks and sprinkle with mint. Serve, passing remaining sauce separately.

SIMPLE SIDES

BRAISED SPRING VEGETABLES

serves 4 to 6

| pressure cook total time 25 minutes | slow cook total time 2 hours 15 minutes |

why this recipe works This vibrant dish of fresh artichokes, asparagus, and peas captures the flavor of springtime with varying textures and verdant colors. Lovely as they are when combined, however, these vegetables don't cook at anywhere near the same rate. The multicooker helped us to cook each to perfection, and in just one pot. First, we pressure or slow cooked halved baby artichokes (in broth to infuse them with flavor). They came out tender and evenly cooked from leaf to stem. We then added asparagus and shelled fresh peas, and simmered them until just crisp-tender. Shredded basil and mint and lemon zest gave the dish an extra bright, springy taste. If you can't find fresh peas, you can substitute 1 cup frozen.

1 lemon, grated to yield 2 teaspoons zest and halved

8 baby artichokes (4 ounces each)

1 tablespoon extra-virgin olive oil, plus extra for serving

3 garlic cloves, minced

¾ cup chicken or vegetable broth

Salt and pepper

1 pound asparagus, trimmed and cut on bias into 2-inch lengths

1 pound fresh peas, shelled (1¼ cups)

2 tablespoons shredded fresh basil

1 tablespoon shredded fresh mint

1 Squeeze zested lemon halves into container filled with 4 cups water, then add spent halves. Working with 1 artichoke at a time, trim stem to about ¾ inch and cut off top quarter of artichoke. Break off bottom 3 or 4 rows of tough outer leaves by pulling them downward. Using paring knife, trim outer layer of stem and base, removing any dark green parts. Cut artichoke in half and submerge in lemon water.

2 Using highest sauté or browning function, cook oil and garlic in multicooker until fragrant, about 1 minute. Remove artichokes from lemon water, shaking off excess liquid, and add to multicooker along with broth and ½ teaspoon salt.

3A to pressure cook Lock lid in place and close pressure release valve. Select high pressure cook function and cook for 4 minutes. Turn off multicooker and quick-release pressure. Carefully remove lid, allowing steam to escape away from you. (If using Instant Pot, quick-release pressure immediately after multicooker reaches pressure.)

3B to slow cook Lock lid in place and open pressure release valve. Select low slow cook function and cook until artichokes are tender, 1 to 2 hours. (If using Instant Pot, select high slow cook function.) Carefully remove lid, allowing steam to escape away from you.

4 Add asparagus and peas and cook using highest sauté or browning function, stirring occasionally, until crisp-tender, 4 to 6 minutes. Turn off multicooker. Stir in basil, mint, and lemon zest, and season with salt and pepper to taste. Transfer vegetables to serving dish and drizzle with extra oil. Serve.

BRAISED CARROTS WITH LEMON AND CHIVES

serves 4 to 6

pressure cook total time 15 minutes	slow cook total time 1 hour 15 minutes

why this recipe works Buttery braised carrots are a classic, well-loved, wonderfully all-purpose side dish, and using the multicooker ensures they come out tender, not mushy, while you focus on the rest of dinner. To make sure the carrots cooked evenly, we cut them into 2-inch lengths and then halved or quartered them lengthwise, depending on thickness, so that all the pieces were of similar size. We cooked them in a small amount of water with some salt and pepper, which seasoned the carrots throughout and accented their natural sweetness. A pat of butter, a spritz of lemon juice, and some fresh chives, added after cooking, gave the carrots richness and brightness. This recipe was developed using carrots with a diameter between 1 and 1½ inches at the thick end. If you are using larger carrots, you may have to cut them into more pieces.

2 pounds carrots, peeled

Salt and pepper

1 tablespoon unsalted butter

1 tablespoon chopped fresh chives

1 teaspoon lemon juice, plus extra for seasoning

1 Cut carrots into 2-inch lengths. Leave thin pieces whole, halve medium pieces lengthwise, and quarter thick pieces lengthwise. Combine carrots, ½ cup water, ½ teaspoon salt, and ⅛ teaspoon pepper in multicooker.

2A to pressure cook Lock lid in place and close pressure release valve. Select high pressure cook function and cook for 3 minutes. (If using Instant Pot, decrease cooking time to 1 minute.) Turn off multicooker and quick-release pressure. Carefully remove lid, allowing steam to escape away from you.

2B to slow cook Lock lid in place and open pressure release valve. Select low slow cook function and cook until carrots are tender, 30 minutes to 1 hour. (If using Instant Pot, select high slow cook function and increase cooking range to 1 to 1½ hours.) Turn off multicooker and carefully remove lid, allowing steam to escape away from you.

3 Stir in butter, chives, and lemon juice. Season with salt, pepper, and extra lemon juice to taste. Serve.

BRAISED CARROTS WITH SCALLIONS AND GINGER
Substitute 1 teaspoon toasted sesame oil for butter, 2 teaspoons rice vinegar for lemon juice, and 2 minced scallions for chives. Stir ½ teaspoon grated fresh ginger into carrots with oil. Season with extra rice vinegar to taste.

GARLICKY BRAISED SWISS CHARD

serves 4 to 6

| pressure cook total time 20 minutes | slow cook total time 2 hours 15 minutes |

why this recipe works Using the multicooker to prepare Swiss chard was a no-brainer—after all, this sturdy green takes well to braising, which turns it meltingly tender and tempers its assertive flavor. We decided on simple flavorings to keep the chard in the spotlight: A healthy dose of garlic and a pinch of red pepper flakes made for a punchy base. We made sure to use the chard stems as well to add textural contrast to our side dish; we cut them into 2-inch lengths and added them to the pot along with the chard leaves. Using broth to braise the greens infused them with extra savory flavor, and, whether pressure or slow cooked, the chard turned out tender with just the right amount of chew. A splash of lemon juice at the end lightened the finished dish.

¼ cup extra-virgin olive oil

5 garlic cloves, sliced thin

⅛ teaspoon red pepper flakes

½ cup chicken or vegetable broth

Salt and pepper

2 pounds Swiss chard, stems cut into 2-inch lengths, leaves sliced into 2-inch-wide strips

1 tablespoon lemon juice, plus extra for seasoning

1 Using highest sauté or browning function, cook 2 tablespoons oil, garlic, and pepper flakes in multicooker until fragrant, about 1 minute. Stir in broth and ¼ teaspoon salt, then stir in chard stems and leaves, 1 handful at a time.

2A to pressure cook Lock lid in place and close pressure release valve. Select high pressure cook function and cook for 5 minutes. Turn off multicooker and quick-release pressure. Carefully remove lid, allowing steam to escape away from you.

2B to slow cook Lock lid in place and open pressure release valve. Select low slow cook function and cook until chard is tender, 1 to 2 hours. (If using Instant Pot, select high slow cook function.) Turn off multicooker and carefully remove lid, allowing steam to escape away from you.

3 Stir in lemon juice and remaining 2 tablespoons oil. Season with salt, pepper, and extra lemon juice to taste. Serve.

GARLICKY BRAISED SWISS CHARD WITH CHORIZO

Using highest sauté or browning function, heat oil in step 1 until shimmering. Add 4 ounces Spanish-style chorizo sausage, quartered lengthwise and sliced thin, and cook until just beginning to brown, about 3 minutes. Stir in garlic, pepper flakes, and ¼ teaspoon smoked paprika and proceed with recipe as directed.

SMASHED POTATOES

serves 4 to 6

pressure cook total time 25 minutes	slow cook total time 3 hours 45 minutes

why this recipe works Bold flavors and a rustic, chunky texture make smashed potatoes a satisfying alternative to mashed. Low-starch, high-moisture potatoes such as Red Bliss were the best choice as their compact structure held up best to cooking and mashing, and their red skins provided nice color. While the potatoes are typically boiled in a pot of water, the multicooker enabled us to cook them in a much smaller amount of liquid, which we turned to our advantage by using a potent mix of broth flavored with butter, garlic, and rosemary. This amped up the richness of the dish and added a subtle, alluring aroma. After cooking, we mashed in ½ cup of cream cheese to give the potatoes some additional creaminess along with a bit of tang to balance out the richness. This recipe was developed using small potatoes with a diameter between 1 and 2 inches. If you are using larger potatoes, you may have to cut them into more pieces. This recipe can be doubled in an 8-quart multicooker.

4 tablespoons unsalted butter

3 garlic cloves, minced

½ teaspoon chopped fresh rosemary

1 bay leaf

2 pounds small red potatoes, unpeeled, halved

½ cup chicken or vegetable broth

Salt and pepper

4 ounces cream cheese, softened

1 Using highest sauté or browning function, melt butter in multicooker. Stir in garlic, rosemary, and bay leaf and cook until fragrant, about 30 seconds. Stir in potatoes, broth, and 1 teaspoon salt.

2A to pressure cook Lock lid in place and close pressure release valve. Select high pressure cook function and cook for 8 minutes. Turn off multicooker and quick-release pressure. Carefully remove lid, allowing steam to escape away from you.

2B to slow cook Lock lid in place and open pressure release valve. Select low slow cook function and cook until potatoes are tender, 2½ to 3½ hours. (If using Instant Pot, select high slow cook function.) Turn off multicooker and carefully remove lid, allowing steam to escape away from you.

3 Discard bay leaf. Add cream cheese and, using potato masher, mash until combined and chunks of potato remain. Season with salt and pepper to taste. Serve.

SMASHED POTATOES WITH HORSERADISH AND CHIVES

Omit rosemary. Mash 2 tablespoons prepared horseradish and 1 tablespoon minced fresh chives into potatoes with cream cheese.

MASHED BUTTERNUT SQUASH WITH SAGE AND TOASTED HAZELNUTS

serves 4 to 6

pressure cook total time 40 minutes	slow cook total time 4 hours 30 minutes

why this recipe works Sweet butternut squash should make for a comforting, autumnal mash, especially when it's laced with earthy sage and fragrant cinnamon. But too often this simple side turns out watery and bland. We turned to our multicooker for a better way. Blooming garlic, onion, and cinnamon in butter gave the dish richness and warm spice flavor. We then stirred in our cut-up squash and a chopped Granny Smith apple, which accented the sweetness of the squash with some bright tang. A small amount of broth steamed the squash and apples to tenderness and boosted flavor, then, after cooking, we simply switched to the sauté function to quickly cook off any excess liquid, concentrating the flavors with minimal effort. Mashing the squash and apples with a potato masher gave the dish a pleasantly rustic texture. Maple syrup and sage stirred in at the end brought just the right balance of earthy sweetness. Chopped hazelnuts added crunch and a nutty finish. This recipe can be doubled in an 8-quart multicooker.

2 tablespoons unsalted butter

½ onion, chopped fine

Salt and pepper

1 garlic clove, minced

⅛ teaspoon ground cinnamon

2 pounds butternut squash, peeled, seeded, and cut into 1-inch pieces (5 cups)

1 Granny Smith apple, peeled, cored, and cut into 1-inch pieces

½ cup chicken or vegetable broth

2 tablespoons maple syrup

2 teaspoons minced fresh sage

¼ cup hazelnuts, toasted, skinned, and chopped coarse

1 Using highest sauté or browning function, melt butter in multicooker. Add onion, 1 teaspoon salt, and ½ teaspoon pepper and cook until onion is softened, 3 to 5 minutes. Stir in garlic and cinnamon and cook until fragrant, about 30 seconds. Stir in squash, apple, and broth.

2A to pressure cook Lock lid in place and close pressure release valve. Select high pressure cook function and cook for 6 minutes. Turn off multicooker and quick-release pressure. Carefully remove lid, allowing steam to escape away from you.

2B to slow cook Lock lid in place and open pressure release valve. Select low slow cook function and cook until squash is tender, 3 to 4 hours. (If using Instant Pot, select high slow cook function.) Carefully remove lid, allowing steam to escape away from you.

3 Using highest sauté or browning function, continue to cook squash mixture, stirring occasionally, until liquid is almost completely evaporated, 3 to 5 minutes. Turn off multicooker. Using potato masher, mash squash mixture until mostly smooth. Stir in maple syrup and sage and season with salt and pepper to taste. Transfer to serving bowl and sprinkle with hazelnuts. Serve.

MASHED BUTTERNUT SQUASH WITH WARM SPICES AND TOASTED ALMONDS

Omit sage. Stir ½ teaspoon ground cumin, ½ teaspoon ground coriander, and ⅛ teaspoon cayenne pepper into multicooker with garlic. Substitute ⅓ cup toasted slivered almonds for hazelnuts.

GREEK-STYLE STEWED ZUCCHINI

serves 6

why this recipe works This ultrasimple recipe combines a few everyday ingredients—zucchini, canned tomatoes, aromatics, and herbs—and transforms them into a savory, satisfying dish. Thanks to the multicooker's moist, concentrated heat, the zucchini became meltingly tender and soft but still held their shape, while the tomato sauce gained deep, bold flavor. Since zucchini naturally contain a lot of water, we started by using the sauté function to brown them in batches, ridding them of some of their excess liquid and giving them a flavor boost. To build our tomato sauce, we started with an aromatic base of onions, garlic, pepper flakes, and oregano. Canned diced tomatoes were the best option for this sauce; tasters liked that the pieces of tomato stayed fairly distinct through either high-heat pressure cooking or extended slow cooking. A smattering of olives, added at the end of cooking so their flavor wouldn't dominate the dish, offered pleasant briny bites. A traditional garnish of shredded fresh mint added a clean, bright finish.

3 tablespoons extra-virgin olive oil, plus extra for drizzling

5 zucchini (8 ounces each), quartered lengthwise, seeded, and cut into 2-inch lengths

1 onion, chopped fine

Salt and pepper

3 garlic cloves, minced

1 teaspoon minced fresh oregano or ¼ teaspoon dried

¼ teaspoon red pepper flakes

1 (28-ounce) can diced tomatoes

2 tablespoons chopped pitted kalamata olives

2 tablespoons shredded fresh mint

1 Using highest sauté or browning function, heat 1 tablespoon oil in multicooker for 5 minutes (or until just smoking). Brown half of zucchini on all sides, 3 to 5 minutes; transfer to bowl. Repeat with 1 tablespoon oil and remaining zucchini; transfer to bowl.

2 Add remaining 1 tablespoon oil, onion, and ¾ teaspoon salt to now-empty multicooker and cook until onion is softened and lightly browned, 5 to 7 minutes. Stir in garlic, oregano, and pepper flakes and cook until fragrant, about 30 seconds. Stir in tomatoes and their juice and zucchini.

3A to pressure cook Lock lid in place and close pressure release valve. Select high pressure cook function and cook for 2 minutes. Turn off multicooker and quick-release pressure. Carefully remove lid, allowing steam to escape away from you.

3B to slow cook Lock lid in place and open pressure release valve. Select low slow cook function and cook until zucchini is tender, 1½ to 2½ hours. (If using Instant Pot, select high slow cook function.) Turn off multicooker and carefully remove lid, allowing steam to escape away from you.

4 If necessary, continue to cook zucchini mixture using highest sauté or browning function until sauce is slightly thickened. Stir in olives and season with salt and pepper to taste. Transfer to serving dish, sprinkle with mint, and drizzle with extra oil. Serve.

PARMESAN RISOTTO

serves 4 to 6

| pressure cook total time 30 minutes | slow cook total time 1 hour 15 minutes |

why this recipe works Risotto is a luxurious dish of perfectly tender Arborio rice in a light, creamy sauce. Traditional versions can be labor-intensive, but with the help of the multicooker's concentrated, moist heat and closed cooking environment, beautifully creamy risotto is achievable even on a weeknight. We started by briefly blooming our aromatics, toasting the rice, and stirring in a bit of wine. A few cups of warm broth gave the rice the proper texture. To pressure cook our risotto, all we had to do was lock on the lid and allow the intense heat to do its work. To slow cook, a couple of small extra steps made for a much better result: We brought the risotto to a simmer so that it was evenly warmed from the start (otherwise, the bottom layer, which was closest to the heating element, cooked through while the top stayed raw), and we topped the rice with parchment to hold in the steam and further ensure that the risotto cooked evenly. Whether we pressure or slow cooked the risotto, the rice turned out perfectly tender with just the right bite. To get the traditional creamy consistency, we encouraged the rice to release additional starch by vigorously stirring in the Parmesan at the end of cooking. Arborio rice, which is high in starch, gives risotto its characteristic creaminess; do not substitute other types of rice here. If using an Instant Pot, do not choose the slow cook function; the rice will not cook through properly.

4 tablespoons unsalted butter

½ onion, chopped fine

Salt

1½ cups Arborio rice

3 garlic cloves, minced

½ cup dry white wine

3 cups chicken broth, warmed, plus extra as needed

2 ounces Parmesan cheese, grated (1 cup)

2 tablespoons minced fresh chives

1 tablespoon lemon juice

1 Using highest sauté or browning function, melt 2 tablespoons butter in multicooker. Add onion and 1 teaspoon salt and cook until onion is softened, 3 to 5 minutes. Stir in rice and garlic and cook until grains are translucent around edges, about 3 minutes. Stir in wine and cook until nearly evaporated, about 1 minute. Stir in warm broth, scraping up any rice that sticks to bottom of pot.

2A to pressure cook Lock lid in place and close pressure release valve. Select high pressure cook function and cook for 7 minutes. Turn off multicooker and quick-release pressure. Carefully remove lid, allowing steam to escape away from you.

2B to slow cook (Do not use Instant Pot to slow cook this recipe.) Bring mixture to simmer using highest sauté or browning function. Gently press 12-inch square sheet of parchment paper onto surface of rice mixture, folding up edges as needed. Lock lid in place and open pressure release valve. Select low slow cook function and cook until rice is tender, 15 to 45 minutes. Turn off multicooker and carefully remove lid, allowing steam to escape away from you.

3 If necessary, adjust consistency with extra hot broth or continue to cook risotto using highest sauté or browning function, stirring frequently, until proper consistency is achieved. (Risotto should be slightly thickened, and spoon dragged along bottom of multicooker should leave trail that quickly fills in.) Add Parmesan and remaining 2 tablespoons butter and stir vigorously until risotto becomes creamy. Stir in chives and lemon juice and season with salt to taste. Serve.

BROWN RICE WITH SHIITAKES AND EDAMAME

serves 6

pressure cook total time 40 minutes	slow cook total time 1 hour 15 minutes

why this recipe works Nutty, hearty brown rice is a great base for a wholesome and flavorful side dish, and using the multicooker made it completely foolproof. We ignored the preset "rice" buttons found on many multicookers, discovering that we got more consistent results by manually setting the pressure or slow cook time ourselves. While rice is usually cooked using the absorption method (in which the rice soaks up all the liquid it's cooked in), we cooked ours in plenty of liquid and then drained away the extra after cooking. This resulted in more evenly cooked rice, since all of the grains were completely submerged in liquid for the whole cooking time. To make our perfect brown rice into a composed side dish, we used the sauté function to cook meaty shiitake mushrooms, fragrant scallions, and some grated fresh ginger, then stirred in edamame for heft and rice vinegar and mirin for brightness.

1½ cups short-grain brown rice, rinsed

Salt

1 tablespoon vegetable oil

4 ounces shiitake mushrooms, stemmed and sliced thin

4 scallions, white parts minced, green parts sliced thin on bias

2 teaspoons grated fresh ginger

1 cup frozen edamame, thawed

4 teaspoons rice vinegar, plus extra for seasoning

1 tablespoon mirin, plus extra for seasoning

1 teaspoon toasted sesame oil

1 Combine 12 cups water, rice, and 2 teaspoons salt in multicooker.

2A to pressure cook Lock lid in place and close pressure release valve. Select high pressure cook function and cook for 8 minutes. Turn off multicooker and let pressure release naturally for 15 minutes. Quick-release any remaining pressure, then carefully remove lid, allowing steam to escape away from you.

2B to slow cook Bring mixture to simmer using highest sauté or browning function. Lock lid in place and open pressure release valve. Select low slow cook function and cook until rice is tender, 20 to 50 minutes. (If using Instant Pot, select high slow cook function.) Turn off multicooker and carefully remove lid, allowing steam to escape away from you.

3 Drain rice and transfer to large bowl. Wipe out multicooker with paper towels. Using highest sauté or browning function, heat vegetable oil in now-empty multicooker until shimmering. Add mushrooms, scallion whites, ginger, and ¼ teaspoon salt and cook until mushrooms are softened, 5 to 7 minutes. Transfer to bowl with rice, then add edamame, vinegar, mirin, sesame oil, and scallion greens and gently toss to combine. Season with extra vinegar and mirin to taste. Serve.

WARM WILD RICE SALAD WITH PECANS AND CRANBERRIES

serves 6

pressure cook total time 40 minutes	slow cook total time 1 hour 30 minutes

why this recipe works Using the multicooker to cook wild rice turned this healthy grain into a hands-off, any-night possibility. When prepared well, wild rice should have a pleasantly chewy outer husk and a nutty, savory flavor; we found that the multicooker could produce perfect rice every time as long as we cooked it in enough water to keep it submerged. The multicooker's ability to moderate the temperature of the cooking liquid meant that every grain turned out tender and intact, whether we cooked it on pressure or slow. A handful of thyme sprigs and a couple of bay leaves added to the water infused the rice with flavor. To transform the nutty rice into a side with contrasting flavors and textures, we added sweet-tart dried cranberries, crunchy pecans, fresh parsley, and bright apple cider vinegar. Do not use quick-cooking or presteamed wild rice in this recipe (read the ingredient list on the package to determine this).

2 cups wild rice, picked over and rinsed

8 sprigs fresh thyme

2 bay leaves

Salt and pepper

1 cup fresh parsley leaves

¾ cup dried cranberries

¾ cup pecans, toasted and chopped coarse

3 tablespoons unsalted butter, melted

1 shallot, minced

2 teaspoons apple cider vinegar

1 Combine 12 cups water, rice, thyme sprigs, bay leaves, and 1 tablespoon salt in multicooker.

2A to pressure cook Lock lid in place and close pressure release valve. Select high pressure cook function and cook for 18 minutes. Turn off multicooker and quick-release pressure. Carefully remove lid, allowing steam to escape away from you.

2B to slow cook Bring mixture to simmer using highest sauté or browning function. Lock lid in place and open pressure release valve. Select low slow cook function and cook until rice is tender, 30 minutes to 1 hour. (If using Instant Pot, select high slow cook function.) Turn off multicooker and carefully remove lid, allowing steam to escape away from you.

3 Discard thyme sprigs and bay leaves. Drain rice and transfer to large bowl. Add parsley, cranberries, pecans, melted butter, shallot, vinegar, and ½ teaspoon salt and gently toss to combine. Season with salt and pepper to taste. Serve.

EGYPTIAN BARLEY SALAD

serves 6

pressure cook total time 1 hour	slow cook total time 2 hours

why this recipe works This impressive and unique salad, inspired by the flavors of Egypt, relies on a bed of tender, toothsome pearl barley as its base. Pearl barley is a great candidate for the multicooker; by cooking the grains in plenty of water, similar to our method for brown rice, they cooked perfectly and evenly. To further ensure separate, intact grains when pressure cooking, we found that a natural release was essential (quick-release caused some of the grains to blow out). After either pressure or slow cooking and then draining the barley, we spread it on a baking sheet so that it would cool quickly. With our perfected barley finished, we incorporated toasty pistachios, tangy pomegranate molasses, and bright, vegetal cilantro, all balanced by warm, earthy spices and sweet golden raisins. Salty feta cheese, pungent scallions, and sweet-tart pomegranate seeds adorned the top of the dish for a colorful and tasty finish. You can find pomegranate molasses in the international aisle of most well-stocked supermarkets. Do not substitute hulled, hull-less, quick-cooking, or presteamed barley (read the ingredient list on the package to determine this).

1½ cups pearl barley

Salt and pepper

3 tablespoons extra-virgin olive oil, plus extra for drizzling

2 tablespoons pomegranate molasses

½ teaspoon ground cinnamon

¼ teaspoon ground cumin

⅓ cup golden raisins

½ cup coarsely chopped fresh cilantro

¼ cup shelled pistachios, toasted and chopped coarse

3 ounces feta cheese, cut into ½-inch cubes (¾ cup)

6 scallions, green parts only, sliced thin

½ cup pomegranate seeds

1 Combine 12 cups water, barley, and 1 tablespoon salt in multicooker.

2A to pressure cook Lock lid in place and close pressure release valve. Select high pressure cook function and cook for 8 minutes. Turn off multicooker and let pressure release naturally for 15 minutes. Quick-release any remaining pressure, then carefully remove lid, allowing steam to escape away from you.

2B to slow cook Bring mixture to simmer using highest sauté or browning function. Lock lid in place and open pressure release valve. Select low slow cook function and cook until barley is tender, 30 minutes to 1½ hours. (If using Instant Pot, select high slow cook function.) Turn off multicooker and carefully remove lid, allowing steam to escape away from you.

3 Drain barley, spread onto rimmed baking sheet, and let cool completely, about 15 minutes. Meanwhile, whisk oil, molasses, cinnamon, cumin, and ½ teaspoon salt together in large bowl. Add cooled barley, raisins, cilantro, and pistachios and gently toss to combine. Season with salt and pepper to taste. Spread barley salad evenly into serving dish and arrange feta, scallions, and pomegranate seeds in separate diagonal rows on top. Drizzle with extra oil and serve.

FRENCH LENTILS WITH CARROTS AND PARSLEY

serves 6

pressure cook total time 1 hour   slow cook total time 2 hours 15 minutes

why this recipe works This simple side has surprisingly complex flavor thanks to toothsome French lentils, or *lentilles du Puy*. These lentils, which are firmer than regular brown or green lentils, are perfect for multicooking since their sturdy texture enables them to stand up well to either the intense or the long, slow heat. To give the lentils classic French flavors, we used the sauté function to cook a traditional *mirepoix* (a mix of carrots, onions, and celery) along with garlic and thyme for aromatic backbone. Using water rather than broth as our cooking liquid let the other flavors come through. We were happy to find that once we locked on the lid, our work was pretty much done. A bit of lemon juice and parsley, added before serving, brightened up the dish. We prefer French green lentils (lentilles du Puy) for this recipe, but it will work with any type of lentils except red or yellow.

2 tablespoons extra-virgin olive oil

2 carrots, peeled and chopped fine

1 onion, chopped fine

1 celery rib, chopped fine

Salt and pepper

2 garlic cloves, minced

1 teaspoon minced fresh thyme or ¼ teaspoon dried

2½ cups water

1 cup French green lentils, picked over and rinsed

2 tablespoons minced fresh parsley

2 teaspoons lemon juice

1 Using highest sauté or browning function, heat 1 tablespoon oil until shimmering. Add carrots, onion, celery, and ½ teaspoon salt and cook until vegetables are softened, 5 to 7 minutes. Stir in garlic and thyme and cook until fragrant, about 30 seconds. Stir in water and lentils.

2A to pressure cook Lock lid in place and close pressure release valve. Select high pressure cook function and cook for 24 minutes. Turn off multicooker and let pressure release naturally for 15 minutes. Quick release any remaining pressure, then carefully remove lid, allowing steam to escape away from you.

2B to slow cook Lock lid in place and open pressure release valve. Select low slow cook function and cook until lentils are tender, 1 to 2 hours. (If using Instant Pot, select high slow cook function.) Turn off multicooker and carefully remove lid, allowing steam to escape away from you.

3 Stir in parsley, lemon juice, and remaining 1 tablespoon oil. Season with salt and pepper to taste. Serve.

BOSTON BAKED BEANS

serves 6

pressure cook total time	slow cook total time
1 hour 30 minutes (plus brining time)	5 hours 30 minutes (plus brining time)

why this recipe works Traditional Boston baked beans consist of tender navy beans napped in a pork- and molasses-enhanced, sweet-savory sauce. Moving the cooking from a low oven (which requires careful adjustment of the cooking liquid in order to get perfectly cooked beans with just the right amount of sauce) to the multicooker made our baked beans bulletproof: The even, steady heat and closed environment (meaning limited evaporation) made this crowd-pleasing dish hands-off. We found that brining the beans made for a much better final product; the cooked beans were well seasoned and held their shape through cooking. Although brining required a bit of advance planning, it couldn't have been simpler, and the next day we merely needed to combine the beans with the rest of the ingredients in the multicooker (and, if slow cooking, bring the mixture to a simmer), and then lock on the lid. You'll get fewer blowouts if you soak the beans overnight, but if you're pressed for time you can quick-salt-soak your beans: In step 1, combine the salt, water, and beans in the multicooker and bring everything to a boil using the highest sauté or browning function. Turn off the multicooker, cover, and let the beans sit for 1 hour. Drain and rinse the beans and proceed with the recipe as directed.

Salt and pepper

1 pound (2½ cups) dried navy beans, picked over and rinsed

6 ounces salt pork, rind removed, rinsed, and cut into 3 pieces

1 onion, halved

½ cup molasses

2 tablespoons packed dark brown sugar

2 tablespoons vegetable oil

1 tablespoon soy sauce

2 teaspoons dry mustard

½ teaspoon baking soda

1 bay leaf

1 Dissolve 1½ tablespoons salt in 8 cups cold water in large container. Add beans and let soak at room temperature for at least 8 hours or up to 24 hours. Drain and rinse well.

2 Combine soaked beans, 2½ cups water, salt pork, onion, molasses, sugar, oil, soy sauce, mustard, 1 teaspoon salt, ½ teaspoon pepper, baking soda, and bay leaf in multicooker.

3A to pressure cook Lock lid in place and close pressure release valve. Select high pressure cook function and cook for 50 minutes. Turn off multicooker and let pressure release naturally for 15 minutes. Quick-release any remaining pressure, then carefully remove lid, allowing steam to escape away from you.

3B to slow cook Bring mixture to simmer using highest sauté or browning function. Gently press 12-inch square sheet of parchment paper onto surface of beans, folding up edges as needed. Lock lid in place and open pressure release valve. Select low slow cook function and cook until beans are tender, 4 to 5 hours. (If using Instant Pot, select high slow cook function and increase cooking range to 5 to 6 hours.) Turn off multicooker and carefully remove lid, allowing steam to escape away from you.

4 Discard bay leaf and onion. If necessary, continue to cook beans using highest sauté or browning function until sauce has thickened and clings to beans. Serve.

DRUNKEN BEANS

serves 6

pressure cook total time	slow cook total time
1 hour 45 minutes (plus brining time)	6 hours 50 minutes (plus brining time)

why this recipe works This satisfying, brothy Mexican dish is humble yet utterly comforting: Dried pinto beans are cooked with a bit of pork or lard, a few herbs and aromatics, and beer or tequila. Since the multicooker had already proven to be a great ally in cooking beans, we set out to create a recipe for creamy, intact beans in a lightly thickened broth with multidimensional (not boozy) flavor. An overnight soak in salt water helped to soften the beans' skins and ensured fewer blowouts, even when cooked under pressure. Bacon gave the dish smoky, savory depth and doubled as a crisp garnish. We sautéed our aromatics—traditional onion, poblano chiles, and garlic—in the rendered bacon fat for deep flavor. A combination of tequila (added before pressure or slow cooking) and light beer (added afterward) created good depth of flavor with subtle malty notes. To underscore the fresh and sweet flavors in the beans, we added a bundle of cilantro sprigs, reserving some of the leaves for garnish. The even heat of the multicooker tenderized the beans and created a velvety broth. You'll get fewer blowouts if you soak the beans overnight, but if you're pressed for time, you can quick-salt-soak your beans: In step 1, combine the salt, water, and beans in the multicooker and bring everything to a boil using the highest sauté or browning function. Turn off the multicooker, cover, and let the beans sit for 1 hour. Drain and rinse the beans and proceed with the recipe as directed. If using an Instant Pot, do not choose the slow cook function; the beans will not cook through properly.

Salt and pepper

1 pound (2½ cups) dried pinto beans, picked over and rinsed

30 sprigs fresh cilantro (1 bunch)

4 slices bacon, cut into ¼-inch pieces

1 onion, chopped fine

2 poblano chiles, stemmed, seeded, and chopped fine

¼ cup tomato paste

3 garlic cloves, minced

½ cup tequila

2 bay leaves

1 cup Mexican lager

2 ounces Cotija cheese, crumbled (½ cup)

Lime wedges

1 Dissolve 1½ tablespoons salt in 8 cups cold water in large container. Add beans and let soak at room temperature for at least 8 hours or up to 24 hours. Drain and rinse well.

2 Pick leaves from 20 cilantro sprigs (reserve stems), chop fine, and refrigerate until needed. Using kitchen twine, tie remaining 10 cilantro sprigs and reserved stems into bundle. Using highest sauté or browning function, cook bacon until rendered and crisp, 10 to 12 minutes. Using slotted spoon, transfer bacon to paper towel–lined bowl; refrigerate until needed.

3 Add onion and poblanos to fat left in multicooker and cook until softened, 5 to 7 minutes. Stir in tomato paste and garlic and cook until fragrant, about 1 minute. Stir in tequila and cook until evaporated, about 2 minutes. Stir in 2 cups water, beans, 1 teaspoon salt, cilantro bundle, and bay leaves.

4A to pressure cook Lock lid in place and close pressure release valve. Select high pressure cook function and cook for 40 minutes. Turn off multicooker and let pressure release

naturally for 15 minutes. Quick-release any remaining pressure, then carefully remove lid, allowing steam to escape away from you.

4B to slow cook (Do not use Instant Pot to slow cook this recipe.) Bring mixture to simmer using highest sauté or browning function. Gently press 12-inch square sheet of parchment paper onto surface of beans, folding up edges as needed.

Lock lid in place and open pressure release valve. Select low slow cook function and cook until beans are tender, 5 to 6 hours. Turn off multicooker and carefully remove lid, allowing steam to escape away from you.

5 Discard bay leaves and cilantro bundle. Stir in beer and bacon, and season with salt and pepper to taste. Serve, passing Cotija, lime wedges, and chopped cilantro separately.

BRAISED CHICKPEAS WITH SAFFRON AND MINT

serves 6

pressure cook total time	slow cook total time
1 hour 10 minutes (plus brining time)	6 hours (plus brining time)

why this recipe works This recipe combines buttery chickpeas with fragrant saffron, plump golden raisins, and fresh mint for a side dish that's as flavorful as it is unique. While we often turn to canned chickpeas for simple sides, the multicooker made cooking dried chickpeas nearly as easy as opening a can—and their flavor and texture couldn't be beat. To make sure the chickpeas were well seasoned and held their shape, we brined them first. We infused the cooking liquid with garlic, onion, and saffron to give the chickpeas nuanced flavor. When slow cooking the beans, we ensured even cooking by bringing the mixture to a simmer and topping the chickpeas with a sheet of parchment before closing the lid. After either pressure or slow cooking, we didn't even need to drain the chickpeas; we simply stirred in the raisins and mint, along with some lemon juice for brightness. A dollop of tangy yogurt offered a creamy finishing touch. You'll get fewer blowouts if you soak the chickpeas overnight, but if you're pressed for time you can quick-salt-soak your chickpeas: In step 1, combine the salt, water, and chickpeas in the multicooker and bring everything to a boil using the highest sauté or browning function. Turn off the multicooker, cover, and let the chickpeas sit for 1 hour. Drain and rinse the chickpeas and proceed with the recipe as directed. If using an Instant Pot, do not choose the slow cook function; the chickpeas will not cook through properly.

Salt and pepper

1 pound (2½ cups) dried chickpeas, picked over and rinsed

3 tablespoons extra-virgin olive oil

1 onion, chopped fine

2 garlic cloves, minced

Pinch saffron threads, crumbled

2 cups chicken or vegetable broth

⅓ cup golden raisins

2 tablespoons chopped fresh mint

2 teaspoons lemon juice

Plain whole-milk yogurt

1 Dissolve 1½ tablespoons salt in 8 cups cold water in large container. Add chickpeas and let soak at room temperature for at least 8 hours or up to 24 hours. Drain and rinse well.

2 Using highest sauté or browning function, heat oil until shimmering. Add onion and ¼ teaspoon salt and cook until onion is softened and lightly browned, 5 to 7 minutes. Stir in garlic and saffron and cook until fragrant, about 30 seconds. Stir in broth and chickpeas.

3A to pressure cook Lock lid in place and close pressure release valve. Select high pressure cook function and cook for 20 minutes. Turn off multicooker and let pressure release naturally for 15 minutes. Quick-release any remaining pressure, then carefully remove lid, allowing steam to escape away from you.

3B to slow cook (Do not use Instant Pot to slow cook this recipe.) Bring mixture to simmer using highest sauté or browning function. Gently press 12-inch square sheet of parchment paper onto surface of chickpeas, folding up edges as needed. Lock lid in place and open pressure release valve. Select low slow cook function and cook until chickpeas are tender, 4½ to 5½ hours. Turn off multicooker and carefully remove lid, allowing steam to escape away from you.

4 Stir in raisins, mint, and lemon juice. Season with salt and pepper to taste. Serve with yogurt.

TEN UNEXPECTED THINGS TO MAKE IN YOUR MULTICOOKER

ALMOND MILK

makes about 4 cups

| pressure cook total time 25 minutes | slow cook total time 3 hours 15 minutes |

why this recipe works Almond milk is a refreshing dairy-free alternative to milk, but much of the almond milk available in stores is loaded with thickeners, stabilizers, and gums. We wanted a simple recipe for almond milk that was healthy and tasted great. Typically, homemade almond milk starts by soaking the almonds for at least 8 hours and up to a full day, but using the multicooker greatly sped up the process, allowing us to skip soaking altogether in favor of pressure cooking for just 1 minute, or slow cooking for a few hours. Afterward, we simply drained the almonds, processed them with some fresh water in a blender (4 cups of water gave our milk the best flavor and texture), and then poured the mixture through a cheesecloth-lined fine-mesh strainer to separate the almond milk from the pulp. Since the pulp still contained a great deal of milk, we squeezed the pulp in the cheesecloth until no liquid remained. To round out the flavor of our almond milk, we added a small amount of salt; some tasters also liked a small amount of sugar. This recipe can be doubled in an 8-quart multicooker.

1¼ cups whole blanched almonds

2 tablespoons sugar (optional)

⅛ teaspoon salt

1 Place almonds in multicooker and add water to cover by 1 inch.

2A to pressure cook Lock lid in place and close pressure release valve. Select high pressure cook function and cook for 1 minute. Turn off multicooker and quick-release pressure. Carefully remove lid, allowing steam to escape away from you.

2B to slow cook Lock lid in place and open pressure release valve. Select low slow cook function and cook until almonds are softened, 2 to 3 hours. (If using Instant Pot, select high slow cook function.) Turn off multicooker and carefully remove lid, allowing steam to escape away from you.

3 Drain almonds and rinse well. Line fine-mesh strainer with triple layer of cheesecloth that overhangs edges and set over large bowl. Process almonds and 4 cups cold water in blender until almonds are finely ground, about 2 minutes. Transfer mixture to prepared strainer and press to extract as much liquid as possible. Gather sides of cheesecloth around almond pulp and gently squeeze remaining milk into bowl; discard spent pulp. Stir in sugar, if using, and salt until completely dissolved. (Almond milk can be refrigerated for up to 2 weeks.)

VANILLA-SPICE ALMOND MILK
Stir 1 teaspoon vanilla extract and 1 teaspoon ground cinnamon into almond milk with salt.

COCONUT-ALMOND MILK
Reduce almonds to 1 cup and add ¾ cup unsweetened shredded coconut to multicooker with almonds.

MULLED CIDER

serves 8 to 10

| pressure cook total time 40 minutes | slow cook total time 3 hours 15 minutes |

why this recipe works Nothing beats a warm mug of mulled cider on a cold fall day. The multicooker thoroughly infused the cider with warm spice notes, whether we used the pressure or the slow cook setting; it also doubled as a serving vessel to keep the cider warm. We made it our goal to accent the sweet-tart apple flavor, not to mask or overwhelm it, so we opted to keep the spices simple. Cinnamon, clove, and allspice offered classic holiday scents, and a surprising addition, black peppercorns, gave the cider a subtle, balanced bite. A knob of ginger and slices of orange and lemon perfumed the cider with bright, fresh notes. Tasters found that, in comparison to stovetop versions, this cider had even more well-rounded flavor since the multicooker drew out all the flavors of our add-ins. If your multicooker has a warming function, feel free to use it for serving in step 3. This recipe can be doubled in an 8-quart multicooker. Serve with cinnamon sticks and orange slices, if desired.

2 quarts apple cider
1 orange, sliced ½ inch thick
½ lemon, sliced ½ inch thick

1 (1-inch) piece ginger, smashed
1 teaspoon allspice berries
5 whole cloves

½ teaspoon black peppercorns
1 cinnamon stick

1 Combine all ingredients in multicooker.

2A to pressure cook Lock lid in place and close pressure release valve. Select high pressure cook function and cook for 1 minute. Turn off multicooker and let pressure release naturally for 15 minutes. Quick-release any remaining pressure, then carefully remove lid, allowing steam to escape away from you.

2B to slow cook Lock lid in place and open pressure release valve. Select low slow cook function and cook until flavors meld, 2 to 3 hours. Turn off multicooker and carefully remove lid, allowing steam to escape away from you.

3 Strain cider through coffee filter–lined fine-mesh strainer into bowl; discard solids. Return cider to now-empty multicooker and keep warm using lowest sauté or browning function. Serve. (Mulled cider can be refrigerated in airtight container for up to 1 week. Reheat before serving.)

APPLESAUCE

makes about 4 cups

pressure cook total time 45 minutes	slow cook total time 4 hours 15 minutes

why this recipe works Homemade applesauce is a great way to showcase the flavor of this fall fruit, and the multicooker was the perfect vessel in which to make it: While stovetop versions require frequent stirring, our multicooker applesauce was fuss-free. We simply peeled, cored, and quartered our apples (Jonagold and Macoun offered the best balance of sweet and tart flavor) and tossed them in the multicooker along with a bit of apple juice or cider to help reinforce (not water down) the apple flavor. Whether we cooked the sauce quickly in the intense heat of the pressure cooker or slowly over several hours on the slow cook setting, our applesauce had great concentrated flavor. An optional cinnamon stick accented the apples with subtle hints of warm spice. While in-season apples were usually plenty sweet on their own, off-season apples benefited from a bit of added sugar after cooking. Empire, Golden Delicious, Jonathan, McIntosh, Pink Lady, and Rome apples also work fairly well in this recipe.

3 pounds Jonagold or Macoun apples, peeled, cored, and quartered

1 cup apple juice or apple cider

1 cinnamon stick (optional)

Pinch salt

Sugar

1 Combine apples, apple juice, cinnamon stick, if using, and salt in multicooker.

2A to pressure cook Lock lid in place and close pressure release valve. Select high pressure cook function and cook for 8 minutes. Turn off multicooker and let pressure release naturally for 15 minutes. Quick-release any remaining pressure, then carefully remove lid, allowing steam to escape away from you.

2B to slow cook Lock lid in place and open pressure release valve. Select low slow cook function and cook until apples are very soft and beginning to disintegrate, 3 to 4 hours. Turn off multicooker and carefully remove lid, allowing steam to escape away from you.

3 Discard cinnamon stick, if using. Using potato masher, mash apple mixture to desired consistency. Season with sugar to taste. Serve warm, at room temperature, or chilled. (Applesauce can be refrigerated in airtight container for up to 1 week.)

GINGER-PEAR SAUCE
Omit cinnamon stick. Substitute Bartlett or Bosc pears for apples. Add 1 (3-inch) piece ginger, cut into ½-inch-thick rounds, to multicooker with pears. Discard ginger rounds before mashing pears.

EASY STRAWBERRY JAM

makes about 2 cups

pressure cook total time	slow cook total time
1 hour (plus cooling and chilling time)	4 hours 30 minutes (plus cooling and chilling time)

why this recipe works The beauty of making jam in the multicooker is how simple it is. You can quickly add your ingredients to the pot and use the pressure or slow cook setting to break down the strawberries, then, with the push of a button, you can simmer the jam down to the perfect consistency. This easy way of cooking jam means you can make small batches; you don't need to invest in bushels of fruit, and there's no need to process jars for long-term storage—you can keep the two jars of jam the recipe makes for up to two months in the fridge. Since we were using berries, which naturally contain pectin, we found that adding extra pectin was unnecessary; some lemon juice and sugar helped our jam set up perfectly. Since acidity can vary from lemon to lemon, we used bottled lemon juice to ensure the right level of acidity in our jam every time. Mashing the cooked strawberries with a potato masher before reducing the jam helped release more pectin and decreased the amount of simmering time needed. The jam will continue to thicken as it cools, so it's best to err on the side of undercooking. Overcooked jam that is dark and thick and that smells of caramelized sugar cannot be saved. This jam cannot be processed for long-term storage.

3 tablespoons bottled lemon juice

1 tablespoon water

1½ pounds strawberries, hulled (5 cups)

1 cup sugar

1 Place 2 small plates in freezer to chill. Combine lemon juice and water in multicooker. Add strawberries, then sprinkle sugar over top.

2A to pressure cook Lock lid in place and close pressure release valve. Select high pressure cook function and cook for 1 minute. Turn off multicooker and let pressure release naturally for 15 minutes. Quick-release any remaining pressure, then carefully remove lid, allowing steam to escape away from you.

2B to slow cook Lock lid in place and open pressure release valve. Select low slow cook function and cook until strawberries are very soft and beginning to disintegrate, 3 to 4 hours. (If using Instant Pot, select high slow cook function.) Turn off multicooker and carefully remove lid, allowing steam to escape away from you.

3 Using potato masher, mash strawberry mixture until strawberries are mostly broken down. Using highest sauté or browning function, cook mixture, stirring often, until thickened and registers 217 to 220 degrees, 10 to 15 minutes. Turn off multicooker.

4 To test consistency, place 1 teaspoon jam on chilled plate and freeze for 2 minutes. Drag your finger through jam on plate; jam has correct consistency when your finger leaves distinct trail. If jam is runny, continue to cook 1 to 3 minutes longer before retesting using second plate. Using large spoon, skim any foam from surface of jam.

5 Meanwhile, place two 1-cup jars in bowl and immerse under hot running water until heated through, 1 to 2 minutes; shake dry. Using funnel and ladle, portion hot jam into hot jars. Let cool completely, cover, and refrigerate until jam is set, 12 to 24 hours. (Jam can be refrigerated for up to 2 months.)

STEEL-CUT OATMEAL

serves 8

why this recipe works We love the chewy texture and fuller flavor of steel-cut oats, but careful monitoring for 40 minutes of stovetop simmering makes them a nonstarter on busy mornings. The multicooker made the process mostly hands-off and guaranteed creamy, hearty steel-cut oatmeal. We first toasted the oats in butter using the sauté function, which brought out their nutty flavor and took only a couple of minutes. Then, we locked on the lid and let the oats pressure or slow cook to tenderness. A bit of salt added to the cooking liquid seasoned them nicely. At the end of cooking, the oats were perfectly chewy, but our oatmeal was on the thin side, and much too hot to eat. Letting the oatmeal sit for 10 minutes before serving solved both problems: The porridge thickened to a pleasantly thick consistency as it cooled. This oatmeal reheats well, so we could easily serve it again later in the week. Serve with your favorite toppings such as brown sugar, butter, maple syrup, cinnamon, dried fruit, and nuts.

2 tablespoons unsalted butter

2 cups steel-cut oats

6 cups water, plus extra as needed

1 teaspoon salt

1 Using highest sauté or browning function, melt butter in multicooker. Add oats and cook, stirring constantly, until golden and fragrant, about 2 minutes. Stir in water and salt.

2A to pressure cook Lock lid in place and close pressure release valve. Select high pressure cook function and cook for 1 minute. Turn off multicooker and let pressure release naturally for 15 minutes. Quick-release any remaining pressure, then carefully remove lid, allowing steam to escape away from you.

2B to slow cook Lock lid in place and open pressure release valve. Select low slow cook function and cook until oats are softened and thickened, 1 to 2 hours. (If using Instant Pot, select high slow cook function.) Turn off multicooker and carefully remove lid, allowing steam to escape away from you.

3 Stir oatmeal to recombine. Remove insert from multicooker and let oatmeal cool for 10 minutes. If necessary, adjust consistency with extra hot water. Serve. (Oatmeal can be refrigerated for up to 4 days. Reheat oatmeal in microwave or in saucepan over medium-low heat; stir often and adjust consistency with hot water as needed.)

BOSTON BROWN BREAD

makes 4 small loaves; serves 6 to 8

pressure cook total time	slow cook total time
1 hour (plus cooling time)	4 hours 30 minutes (plus cooling time)

why this recipe works Rich with the flavors of molasses and whole grains, classic New England brown bread is made by pouring batter into cans and then steaming the cans in a water bath on the stovetop. Using the multicooker was a fuss-free way to re-create this steamy environment, producing supremely moist loaves. A combination of whole-wheat flour, rye flour, and finely ground cornmeal gave our bread balanced whole-grain flavor. Baking soda and baking powder lightened the bread's texture, and melted butter offered richness. We lined the multicooker insert with parchment to prevent the metal cans from staining it, and poured in some water to create steam. When pressure cooking, we found it was best to use low pressure to ensure our loaves had appropriately flat ends; high pressure caused the batter to puff too much. We prefer Quaker White Cornmeal in this recipe, though other types will work; do not use coarse grits. Any style of molasses will work except blackstrap. You will need four empty 15-ounce cans for this recipe. Use cans that are labeled BPA-free. Brown bread is great as is or toasted and buttered.

¾ cup (4⅛ ounces) rye flour

¾ cup (4⅛ ounces) whole-wheat flour

¾ cup (3¾ ounces) fine white cornmeal

1¾ teaspoons baking soda

½ teaspoon baking powder

1 teaspoon salt

1⅔ cups buttermilk

½ cup molasses

3 tablespoons butter, melted and cooled slightly

¾ cup raisins

1 Fold four 12 by 8-inch pieces of aluminum foil in half twice to yield rectangles that measure 6 by 4 inches, and grease 1 side with vegetable oil spray. Coat inside of 4 clean 15-ounce cans with oil spray.

2 Whisk rye flour, whole-wheat flour, cornmeal, baking soda, baking powder, and salt together in large bowl. Whisk buttermilk, molasses, and melted butter together in second bowl. Stir raisins into buttermilk mixture. Add buttermilk mixture to flour mixture and stir until combined and no dry flour remains. Divide batter evenly among prepared cans and smooth top with back of greased spoon. Wrap tops of cans tightly with prepared foil, greased side facing batter.

3 Line bottom of multicooker with parchment paper. Add water to multicooker until it reaches about ½ inch up sides of insert (about 2 cups water), then set cans in multicooker.

4A to pressure cook Lock lid in place and close pressure release valve. Select low pressure cook function and cook for 20 minutes. Turn off multicooker and let pressure release naturally for 15 minutes. Quick-release any remaining pressure, then carefully remove lid, allowing steam to escape away from you.

4B to slow cook Lock lid in place and open pressure release valve. Select low slow cook function and cook until skewer inserted in center of loaves comes out clean, 3 to 4 hours. (If using Instant Pot, select high slow cook function.) Turn off multicooker and carefully remove lid, allowing steam to escape away from you.

5 Using tongs and sturdy spatula, transfer cans to wire rack and let cool, uncovered, for 20 minutes. Invert cans and slide loaves onto rack and let cool completely, about 1 hour. Slice and serve. (Bread can be wrapped tightly in plastic wrap and stored at room temperature for up to 3 days.)

BUFFALO CHICKEN WINGS

serves 6

| pressure cook total time 1 hour | slow cook total time 2 hours 45 minutes |

why this recipe works Great wings should boast juicy, tender meat and a crisp coating. You might not think of making them in your multicooker, but this appliance turned out to be the perfect all-in-one vessel for this crowd-pleasing bar snack. Both pressure and slow cooking the wings did a great job rendering excess fat and producing perfectly tender, fall-off-the-bone meat. Using hot sauce as our cooking liquid infused the wings with great flavor from the outset. But while our wings were emerging amazingly juicy and flavorful, they lacked the hallmark crisp exteriors of truly great wings. Frying is the best way to get the crunch we were after, but monitoring the temperature of the oil can be difficult. Then it occurred to us that the multicooker has a temperature regulator built right in: The heating element is designed to reach a specific temperature on each setting. It reaches this temperature quickly, then self-regulates to maintain the heat—which means there's no need for the cook to babysit a thermometer or fuss with stovetop burners. The highest sauté or browning function reaches a temperature that's perfect for frying (between 325 and 350 degrees), so we used it to heat just enough oil to submerge the wings in batches. Once the oil came up to temperature, we fried the wings and were happy to find that the high sides of the pot also prevented the oil from splattering and making a mess. Finally, we tossed our crisp, golden-brown wings with a classic Buffalo sauce that we quickly stirred together using a combination of Frank's RedHot sauce and Tabasco for extra kick. We deepened the sauce's flavor by adding brown sugar and cider vinegar. With a homemade blue cheese dressing served alongside, our foolproof multicooker wings were complete. Serve with celery and carrot sticks.

creamy blue cheese dressing

2½ ounces blue cheese, crumbled (½ cup)

3 tablespoons buttermilk

3 tablespoons sour cream

2 tablespoons mayonnaise

2 teaspoons white wine vinegar

Salt and pepper

wings

3 pounds chicken wings, cut at joints, wingtips discarded

1 cup hot sauce, preferably Frank's RedHot Original Cayenne Pepper Sauce

4 cups vegetable oil

4 tablespoons unsalted butter, melted

2 tablespoons Tabasco sauce or other hot sauce

1 tablespoon packed dark brown sugar

2 teaspoons cider vinegar

1 for the creamy blue cheese dressing Mash blue cheese and buttermilk in small bowl with fork until mixture resembles cottage cheese with small curds. Stir in sour cream, mayonnaise, and vinegar, and season with salt and pepper to taste. Cover and refrigerate until ready to serve. (Dressing can be refrigerated for up to 4 days.)

2 for the wings Combine chicken wings and ½ cup hot sauce in multicooker.

7A to pressure cook Lock lid in place and close pressure release valve. Select high pressure cook function and cook for 5 minutes. Turn off multicooker and quick-release pressure. Carefully remove lid, allowing steam to escape away from you.

3B to slow cook Lock lid in place and open pressure release valve. Select low slow cook function and cook until wings are tender, 1 to 2 hours. (If using Instant Pot, select high slow cook function.) Turn off multicooker and carefully remove lid, allowing steam to escape away from you.

4 Adjust oven rack to middle position and heat oven to 200 degrees. Set wire rack in rimmed baking sheet. Using slotted spoon, transfer wings to paper towel–lined plate and pat dry with paper towels. Discard cooking liquid and wipe multicooker clean with additional paper towels.

5 Using highest sauté or browning function, heat oil in now-empty multicooker until it registers between 325 and 350 degrees. Carefully place one-third of wings in oil and cook until golden and crisp, 8 to 10 minutes, turning halfway through cooking. (If using Instant Pot, increase cooking time to about 15 minutes.) Using slotted spoon, place wings on prepared sheet and keep warm in oven. Return oil to 325 to 350 degrees and repeat with remaining wings in 2 batches.

6 Whisk melted butter, Tabasco, sugar, vinegar, and remaining ½ cup hot sauce together in large bowl. Add wings and toss to coat. Serve immediately.

MUSSELS WITH WHITE WINE AND GARLIC

serves 4 to 6

pressure cook total time 20 minutes	slow cook total time 50 minutes

why this recipe works Paired with some crusty bread and a simple salad, mussels make a lovely light meal. But getting them perfectly cooked can be tricky, with most stovetop recipes inevitably turning out some overcooked and some undercooked mussels. We made cooking mussels absolutely foolproof by using our multicooker, which evenly surrounded the mussels with steam and resulted in a pot full of tender, plump mussels every time. On the pressure setting, we needed to cook the mussels for just 1 minute; on the slow cook setting (which heats up much faster than a traditional slow cooker) the mussels were cooked perfectly within half an hour. To infuse the mussels with lots of flavor, we sautéed garlic, thyme, and red pepper flakes in butter, and used wine as the cooking liquid. We finished the mussels with a sprinkle of fresh parsley. You can substitute 3 pounds of littleneck clams for the mussels; increase the pressure cooking time to 2 minutes. Discard any raw mussels with an unpleasant odor or with a cracked or broken shell or a shell that won't close. Serve with crusty bread.

4 tablespoons unsalted butter

4 garlic cloves, sliced thin

4 sprigs fresh thyme

¼ teaspoon salt

Pinch red pepper flakes

2 bay leaves

3 pounds mussels, scrubbed and debearded

½ cup dry white wine

2 tablespoons minced fresh parsley

1 Using highest sauté or browning function, melt butter in multicooker. Add garlic, thyme sprigs, salt, pepper flakes, and bay leaves and cook until fragrant, about 30 seconds. Stir in mussels and wine.

2A to pressure cook Lock lid in place and close pressure release valve. Select high pressure cook function and cook for 1 minute. Turn off multicooker and quick-release pressure. Carefully remove lid, allowing steam to escape away from you.

2B to slow cook Lock lid in place and open pressure release valve. Select low slow cook function and cook until mussels open, 15 to 20 minutes. (If using Instant Pot, select high slow cook function.) Turn off multicooker and carefully remove lid, allowing steam to escape away from you.

3 Discard thyme sprigs, bay leaves, and any mussels that have not opened. Stir in parsley and transfer to large serving bowl. Serve.

FLAN

serves 4 to 6

why this recipe works Flan is a classic Spanish dessert, slightly sweeter than a traditional baked custard, with a crowning touch of thin, sweet caramel that pools over the dish once unmolded. Flan is often baked in a water bath to ensure a silky-smooth texture, so we knew the moist, enclosed environment of the multicooker would be a promising way to make this recipe foolproof. We started with the caramel layer. We hoped we could make the caramel directly in the multicooker insert, but this resulted in a sticky mess—it was far easier and more efficient simply to make the caramel on the stove, where we could monitor its color and doneness. For the custard, we used a base of sweetened condensed milk and whole milk for richness and balanced sweetness. Mixing the dairy with a combination of whole eggs and egg yolks resulted in a tender, silky custard. We poured the caramel and the custard into a 6-inch cake pan, which fit nicely into the multicooker insert, and covered it with foil so the top wouldn't be marred by any drips. We also placed a foil sling under the cake pan for easy removal from the multicooker. The low pressure setting and the low slow cook setting both offered a gentle cooking environment that produced a smooth, velvety custard every time. You will need a 6-inch round cake pan for this recipe. If using the slow cook function, begin checking the temperature of the custard after 45 minutes and continue to monitor it until it is done. Serve the flan on a dish with a raised rim to contain the liquid caramel.

⅔ cup (4⅔ ounces) sugar

2 large eggs plus 2 large yolks

1 cup whole milk

1 cup sweetened condensed milk

⅛ teaspoon grated lemon zest

1 Place ¼ cup water in large saucepan. Pour sugar into center of saucepan, taking care not to let sugar crystals touch saucepan sides. Gently stir with spatula to moisten sugar thoroughly. Bring to boil over medium heat and cook, without stirring, until mixture is straw-colored, 4 to 7 minutes. Gently swirling saucepan, continue to cook until sugar is reddish-amber and fragrant, 1 to 2 minutes.

2 Immediately remove saucepan from heat, add 2 tablespoons water (mixture will bubble), and swirl saucepan until water is incorporated. Pour caramel into 6-inch round cake pan; do not scrape out saucepan.

3 Whisk eggs and yolks together in bowl. Whisk in milk, condensed milk, and lemon zest until incorporated, then pour into pan with caramel and cover with aluminum foil. Fold second sheet of foil into 12 by 9-inch sling. Press sling into multicooker, allowing narrow ends to rest along sides of insert. Add water to multicooker until it reaches about ½ inch up sides of insert (about 2 cups). Set pan in multicooker on top of foil sling.

4A to pressure cook Lock lid in place and close pressure release valve. Select low pressure cook function and cook for 15 minutes. (If using Instant Pot, decrease cooking time to 10 minutes.) Turn off multicooker and let pressure release

naturally for 30 minutes. Quick-release any remaining pressure, then carefully remove lid, allowing steam to escape away from you.

4B to slow cook Lock lid in place and open pressure release valve. Select low slow cook function and cook until flan registers 180 degrees, 45 minutes to 1 hour 15 minutes. (If using Instant Pot, select high slow cook function.) Turn off multicooker and carefully remove lid, allowing steam to escape away from you.

5 Using sling, transfer pan to wire rack and let cool to room temperature, about 2 hours. Cover with plastic wrap and refrigerate until well chilled, at least 3 hours or up to 3 days.

6 To serve, slide paring knife around edges of pan. Invert serving dish on top of pan, and turn pan and dish over. When flan is released, remove pan. Use rubber spatula to scrape residual caramel onto flan. Slice and serve.

CHEESECAKE

serves 8

pressure cook total time	slow cook total time
2 hours (plus cooling and chilling time)	4 hours (plus cooling and chilling time)

why this recipe works Cheesecake may not be the first thing you think of when you think of your multicooker, but the moist cooking environment is ideal for this notoriously tricky dessert, since it helps prevent the cheesecake from drying out and cracking. We set our sights on developing a foolproof recipe that could be pressure or slow cooked and would boast all the sweet creaminess we expect from a great cheesecake. We whipped up a simple graham cracker crust and a rich filling using our food processor for ease and speed. When it came time to cook the cheesecake, we discovered a few secrets to success. First, we covered the cheesecake with foil so that any condensation in the pot wouldn't drip down and mar the cake's surface. Next, we created a steamy environment by adding water to the bottom of the multicooker, raising the springform pan above the water using a foil ring. And finally, we honed in on specific settings: We found that, when pressure cooking, the low pressure setting produced a cheesecake with a better texture than when we used the high pressure setting, which caused the cake to puff and curdle. Letting the pressure release naturally for 30 minutes allowed the cake to finish cooking gently in the residual heat. Similarly, when using the slow cook function, we went with the low setting, then let the cake rest in the covered (but turned-off) multicooker for an hour. No matter which method we chose, our cheesecake emerged perfectly creamy and with nary a crack. This recipe was developed using an 8-quart multicooker. If using the pressure cook function on a 6-quart multicooker, increase the cooking time to 40 minutes (if using an Instant Pot, increase the cooking time to 50 minutes). You will need a 6-inch springform pan for this recipe. If your multicooker comes with a rack, you can use it instead of the foil ring in step 3. To make neat slices, dip the knife into hot water and wipe it clean after each cut. Serve with Strawberry Topping (recipe follows) if desired.

6 whole graham crackers, broken into 1-inch pieces

2 tablespoons unsalted butter, melted and cooled

1 tablespoon plus ⅔ cup (4⅔ ounces) sugar

½ teaspoon ground cinnamon

Salt

18 ounces cream cheese, softened

1 teaspoon vanilla extract

¼ cup sour cream

2 large eggs, room temperature

1 Pulse cracker pieces in food processor to fine crumbs, about 20 pulses. Add melted butter, 1 tablespoon sugar, cinnamon, and pinch salt and pulse to combine, about 4 pulses. Sprinkle crumbs into 6-inch springform pan and press into even layer using bottom of dry measuring cup. Wipe out processor bowl.

2 Process cream cheese, vanilla, ¼ teaspoon salt, and remaining ⅔ cup sugar in now-empty processor until combined, about 15 seconds, scraping down sides of bowl as needed. Add sour cream and eggs and process until just incorporated, about 15 seconds; do not overmix. Pour filling over crust in pan, smooth top, and cover with aluminum foil.

3 Add water to multicooker until it reaches about ½ inch up sides of insert (about 2 cups). Loosely roll 24 by 12-inch piece foil widthwise into 1-inch cylinder, then bend cylinder to form 5-inch ring. Place foil ring in center of multicooker and set pan on top.

4A to pressure cook Lock lid in place and close pressure release valve. Select low pressure cook function and cook for 30 minutes. (If using Instant Pot, decrease cooking time to 25 minutes.) Turn off multicooker and let pressure release naturally for 30 minutes. Quick-release any remaining pressure, then carefully remove lid, allowing steam to escape away from you.

4B to slow cook Lock lid in place and open pressure release valve. Select low slow cook function and cook until cheesecake registers 150 degrees, 1 to 2 hours. (If using Instant Pot, select high slow cook function.) Turn off multicooker and let cheesecake sit, covered, for 1 hour.

5 Transfer cheesecake to wire rack and discard foil cover. Run small knife around edge of cake and gently blot away condensation using paper towels. Let cheesecake cool in pan to room temperature, about 1 hour. Cover with plastic wrap and refrigerate until well chilled, at least 3 hours or up to 3 days.

6 About 30 minutes before serving, run small knife around edge of cheesecake, then remove sides of pan. Invert cheesecake onto sheet of parchment paper, then turn cheesecake right side up onto serving dish. Serve.

STRAWBERRY TOPPING

Using potato masher, mash 8 ounces hulled strawberries in bowl into paste. Stir in 12 ounces hulled and sliced strawberries and 3 tablespoons sugar and let sit at room temperature until sugar has dissolved and berries are juicy, at least 30 minutes or up to 2 hours. Makes about 2 cups.

CONVERSIONS AND EQUIVALENTS

Some say cooking is a science and an art. We would say that geography has a hand in it, too. Flours and sugars manufactured in the United Kingdom and elsewhere will feel and taste different from those manufactured in the United States. So we cannot promise that the loaf of bread you bake in Canada or England will taste the same as a loaf baked in the States, but we can offer guidelines for converting weights and measures. We also recommend that you rely on your instincts when making our recipes. Refer to the visual cues provided. If the dough hasn't "come together in a ball" as described, you may need to add more flour—even if the recipe doesn't tell you to. You be the judge.

The recipes in this book were developed using standard U.S. measures following U.S. government guidelines. The charts below offer equivalents for U.S. and metric measures. All conversions are approximate and have been rounded up or down to the nearest whole number.

Example

1 teaspoon	=	4.9292 milliliters, rounded up to 5 milliliters
1 ounce	=	28.3495 grams, rounded down to 28 grams

Volume Conversions

U.S.	METRIC
1 teaspoon	5 milliliters
2 teaspoons	10 milliliters
1 tablespoon	15 milliliters
2 tablespoons	30 milliliters
¼ cup	59 milliliters
⅓ cup	79 milliliters
½ cup	118 milliliters
¾ cup	177 milliliters
1 cup	237 milliliters
1¼ cups	296 milliliters
1½ cups	355 milliliters
2 cups (1 pint)	473 milliliters
2½ cups	591 milliliters
3 cups	710 milliliters
4 cups (1 quart)	0.946 liter
1.06 quarts	1 liter
4 quarts (1 gallon)	3.8 liters

Weight Conversions

OUNCES	GRAMS
½	14
¾	21
1	28
1½	43
2	57
2½	71
3	85
3½	99
4	113
4½	128
5	142
6	170
7	198
8	227
9	255
10	283
12	340
16 (1 pound)	454

Conversions for Common Baking Ingredients

Baking is an exacting science. Because measuring by weight is far more accurate than measuring by volume, and thus more likely to produce reliable results, in our recipes we provide ounce measures in addition to cup measures for many ingredients. Refer to the chart below to convert these measures into grams.

INGREDIENT	OUNCES	GRAMS
flour		
1 cup all-purpose flour*	5	142
1 cup cake flour	4	113
1 cup whole-wheat flour	5½	156
sugar		
1 cup granulated (white) sugar	7	198
1 cup packed brown sugar (light or dark)	7	198
1 cup confectioners' sugar	4	113
cocoa powder		
1 cup cocoa powder	3	85
butter†		
4 tablespoons (½ stick or ¼ cup)	2	57
8 tablespoons (1 stick or ½ cup)	4	113
16 tablespoons (2 sticks or 1 cup)	8	227

* U.S. all-purpose flour, the most frequently used flour in this book, does not contain leaveners, as some European flours do. These leavened flours are called self-rising or self-raising. If you are using self-rising flour, take this into consideration before adding leaveners to a recipe.

† In the United States, butter is sold both salted and unsalted. We generally recommend unsalted butter. If you are using salted butter, take this into consideration before adding salt to a recipe.

Oven Temperatures

FAHRENHEIT	CELSIUS	GAS MARK
225	105	¼
250	120	½
275	135	1
300	150	2
325	165	3
350	180	4
375	190	5
400	200	6
425	220	7
450	230	8
475	245	9

Converting Temperatures from an Instant-Read Thermometer

We include doneness temperatures in many of the recipes in this book. We recommend an instant-read thermometer for the job. Refer to the table above to convert Fahrenheit degrees to Celsius. Or, for temperatures not represented in the chart, use this simple formula:

Subtract 32 degrees from the Fahrenheit reading, then divide the result by 1.8 to find the Celsius reading.

Example:
"Roast chicken until thighs register 175 degrees."
To convert:

$$175°F - 32 = 143°$$
$$143° \div 1.8 = 79.44°C, \text{ rounded down to } 79°C$$

INDEX

Note: Page references in *italics* indicate photographs.